17.06
10/91

Crosscurrents / Modern Critiques / New Series

James Gould Cozzens: New Acquist of True Experience
Edited by Matthew J. Bruccoli

Thomas Pynchon: The Art of Allusion
By David Cowart

Twentieth-Century American Literary Naturalism: An Interpretation
By Donald Pizer

John Gardner: Critical Perspectives
Edited by Robert A. Morace and Kathryn VanSpanckeren

Robert Coover: The Universal Fictionmaking Process
By Lois Gordon

Margaret Drabble: Existing Within Structures
By Mary Hurley Moran

The Fiction of Philip Roth and John Updike
By George J. Searles

Donald Pizer

REALISM and NATURALISM in NINETEENTH-CENTURY AMERICAN LITERATURE

Revised Edition

Southern Illinois University Press
CARBONDALE AND EDWARDSVILLE

Copyright © 1984 by the Board of Trustees,
Southern Illinois University

Printed in the United States of America
Edited by Dennis M. Osborne
Designed by Bob Nance
Production supervised by Kathleen Giencke

Permission to reprint "Theodore Dreiser's 'Nigger Jeff'" has been granted by
Duke University Press. Copyright © 1969 by Duke Univ. Press.

"Jack London: The Problem of Form" first appeared in *Studies in the Literary Imagination*, vol. 16, no. 2. Reprinted by permission.

Library of Congress Cataloging in Publication Data

Pizer, Donald.
    Realism and naturalism in nineteenth-century American literature.
    (Crosscurrents/modern critiques/new series)
    Bibliography: p.
    Includes index.
    1. American fiction—19th century—History and criticism—Addresses, es-
says, lectures. 2. Realism in literature—Addresses, essays, lectures. 3. Naturalism in literature—Addresses, essays, lectures. I. Title. II. Series: Crosscurrents/
modern critiques. New series. PS377.P5   1984   810'.9'12   83-20406
ISBN 0-8093-1125-9

87 86 85 84   4 3 2 1

For Leon Howard

Contents

Preface to the Second Edition   ix

Introduction   xi

1   Late Nineteenth-Century American Realism   1

2   Late Nineteenth-Century American Naturalism   9

3   Nineteenth-Century American Naturalism: An
Approach Through Form   31

4   American Literary Naturalism: The Example of
Dreiser   41

5   The Problem of Philosophy in the Naturalistic
Novel   59

6   The Evolutionary Foundation of W. D. Howells's
Criticism and Fiction   70

7   Evolutionary Ideas in Late Nineteenth-Century English and American Literary Criticism   86

8   Hamlin Garland and Stephen Crane: The Naturalist as Romantic Individualist   96

9   Frank Norris's Definition of Naturalism   107

10   The Significance of Frank Norris's Literary Criticism   112

11   The Ethical Unity of *The Rise of Silas Lapham*   121

12   Hamlin Garland's 1891 *Main-Travelled Roads*: Local Color as Art   127

13   Stephen Crane's *Maggie* and American Naturalism   143

14   Synthetic Criticism and Frank Norris's *The Octopus*   154

15   Jack London: The Problem of Form   166

16   Theodore Dreiser's "Nigger Jeff": The Development of an Aesthetic   180

Notes   197

Bibliography   217

Index   223

Preface to
The Second Edition

THE WIDESPREAD USE of the 1966 edition of this collection of essays about late nineteenth-century American literature has led me to believe that a revised edition, containing both the heart of the original book and considerable new material reflecting my continuing thinking on the subject, might serve a similar purpose. The revision has taken two forms: omission of three essays from the 1966 edition and inclusion of six new ones; and minor revision of the text and notes of the remaining 1966 essays (as well as the Bibliography), principally to bring this material up to date. For the interested reader, the three essays from the 1966 edition which have been omitted are: "Evolution and Criticism: Thomas Sergeant Perry," "Evolutionary Criticism and the Defense of Howellsian Realism," and "The Garland-Crane Relationship." The six essays which have been added are: "American Literary Naturalism: An Approach Through Form," "American Literary Naturalism: The Example of Dreiser," "The Problem of Philosophy in the Naturalistic Novel," "Hamlin Garland's 1891 *Main-Travelled Roads*: Local Color as Art," "Jack London: The Problem of Form," and "Dreiser's 'Nigger Jeff': The Development of an Aesthetic."

I wish to thank the editors of the following journals for permission to republish: *American Literature* ("The Ethical Unity of *The Rise of Silas Lapham*," "Synthetic Criticism and Frank Norris's *The Octopus*," and "Dreiser's 'Nigger Jeff': The Development of an Aesthetic"); *American Quarterly* ("Hamlin Garland and Stephen Crane: The Naturalist as Romantic Individualist"); *Bucknell Review* ("Late Nineteenth-Century American Naturalism" and "The Problem of Philosophy in the Naturalistic Novel"); *Criticism* ("Stephen Crane's *Maggie* and American Naturalism"); *Forum* (Houston) ("American Literary Naturalism: An Approach Through Form"); *Journal of Aesthetics and Art Criticism* ("Evolutionary Ideas and Late Nineteenth-Century English and American Literary Criticism"); *Modern Fiction Studies* (Frank Norris's Definition of Naturalism"); *Nineteenth Century Fiction* ("Late Nineteenth-Century American Realism"); *Philological Quarterly* ("The Evolutionary Foundation of W. D. Howells's *Criticism and Fiction*"); *Studies in American Fiction* ("American Literary Naturalism: The Example of Dreiser"); and *Studies in the Literary Imagination* ("Jack London: The Problem of Form"). I wish also to thank the University of Texas Press for permission to republish paragraphs which appeared originally in my edition of *The Literary Criticism of Frank Norris* ("The Significance of Frank Norris's Literary Criticism"). The essay on Hamlin Garland's *Main-Travelled Roads* appeared originally as the Introduction to my edition of the collection of stories published by Charles E. Merrill Publishing Company.

Introduction

THIS BOOK ATTEMPTS to answer two major questions: how can one best describe realism and naturalism in nineteenth-century American fiction, and what is the relationship between the literary criticism of the age and the emergence and nature of realism and naturalism? The first ten chapters deal more or less directly with these questions. Although the last six chapters of the book are devoted primarily to independent interpretations of particular works of fiction, these interpretations indirectly support the conclusions reached earlier. My method is therefore that of a selective and frequently incomplete examination of particular works of fiction and literary criticism. I wish to suggest some of the basic tendencies in late nineteenth-century American fiction and criticism rather than to attempt a description of the period as a whole.

Perhaps I can best summarize my ideas about these tendencies by beginning with the clichés that the literature of the age combined the old and the new and that it looked both backward and forward. The old consisted of a faith in man's

worth and freedom, in his power to choose even if he frequently did not choose well. The vestiges of this affirmative view of
man's nature and potential are responsible for much of the thematic complexity in late nineteenth-century American fiction.
The realists of the seventies and eighties and the naturalists of
the nineties reflected in their novels their age's increasing
sense of the limitations imposed upon man by his biological
past and his social present. But they also persisted—at first
confidently and openly, later hesitantly and obliquely—in
dramatizing man as a creature of significance and worth.
Whether in a Huck Finn beleaguered by a socially corrupted
conscience yet possessed of a good heart, or a Carrie grasping
for the material plenty of life yet reaching beyond as well, in
these and other works the late nineteenth-century American
realists and naturalists continued to maintain the tension between actuality and hope which in its various forms has characterized most Western literature since the Renaissance.

The realistic or naturalistic novel is thus not a detached
and objective account of the destruction of the individual by
material force. Nor are these novels composed of slabs of the
commonplace and trivial in experience. Beginning with
Twain and James, and continuing more strongly and fully in
Norris, Crane, and Dreiser, the novelist depicts life as extraordinary and sensational rather than as placid and commonplace. The first generation of late nineteenth-century
novelists dramatized the validity of older faiths in areas
of contemporary and local experience recently legitimatized
for fictional representation. The increasingly profound involvement of the second generation of novelists in all ranges
of life led them to that combination of violent action and degrading detail organized around implicit but oblique systems
of value which constitutes the modern tragic vision. Thus,
late nineteenth-century fiction is not a long and dull hiatus

between the romances of Hawthorne and Melville and those of Faulkner, as much criticism of American fiction implies. It rather moves toward and eventually embodies the intermingling of the commonplace and the sensational, and of the humanly ennobling and the humanly degrading, which characterizes much of contemporary American fiction.

I have therefore approached late nineteenth-century fiction as though it were something more than the minor details of life sketched in accordance with superficial literary and philosophical formulas. I have been much more summary and boldly analytical in discussing the literary criticism of the age, both because criticism itself is inherently more ideological than fiction and because much of the criticism was argumentative. In general, this criticism—though not as important as either the fiction of the period or the criticism of other periods—is significant because of its role in the rise of realism and because it reflects some of the same tendencies present in fiction. Here is the naive and often dreary application of evolutionary ideas to literature in order to defend or advocate realism. But here also is the continuation in Garland's and Crane's romantic individualism and in Norris's primitivism of a critical subjectivism which stressed above all the truthfulness of an artist's personal vision of life. Here again, therefore, are the outer and inner realities: the crude determinism of impersonal evolutionary law juxtaposed against a faith in a private vision. As in the fiction of the age, these two views do not so much clash as complement each other in a conception of literature and life which is awkwardly complex rather than comfortably obvious.

The large effect of these studies should be to encourage the view that the literature of late nineteenth-century America is not so simple as it sometimes appears to be. The last group of specialized studies confirms this position, for each chapter rejects a conventional simplistic interpretation of a standard fictional work of the age—that, for example, *The Rise of Silas Lapham* is marred by its double plot, or that *Maggie* is a superficial study of environmental determinism, or that *The Octopus* can be successfully interpreted by relating its symbols to a cultural myth. The tone of many of the studies in this volume is frequently the scholarly and polemical one of certainty and finality. But the impression I really wish to impart is that late nineteenth-century American literature is still, despite considerable work during the last several decades, for the most part unexplored, and that much remains to be done both in the restudy of works buried under older reductive generalizations and in the shaping of new general ideas about the complex patterns of theme and form which emerge out of this and any age's serious attempt to render its values and experience in art.

Realism and Naturalism in

Nineteenth-Century American Literature

1
Late Nineteenth-Century American Realism

CRITICS AND LITERARY historians of all persua-
sions have found that such broad descriptive terms as
classicism, romanticism, and realism are valuable and necessary despite their multiple meanings. To describe a writer,
work, theme, or genre as classic, romantic, or realistic is to
employ a useful frame of reference whence further examination and discussion may proceed. What is required, of
course, is some general agreement on the frame of reference,
and for the past several decades there have been frequent attempts to sharpen our awareness of the full implications of
the terms classicism and romanticism. Realism, as a more recent, seemingly less complicated literary mode, has had less
such attention devoted to it. Indeed, George J. Becker's essay
in *Modern Language Quarterly* over thirty years ago has been
one of the few notable attempts to define realism.[1] Becker,
basing his definition upon European and American fiction
since approximately 1870, listed three criteria of the realistic
mode. The first is verisimilitude of detail derived from observation and documentation. The second is an effort to ap-

proach the norm of experience—that is, a reliance upon the representative rather than the exceptional in plot, setting, and character. The last is an objective, so far as an artist can achieve objectivity, rather than a subjective or idealistic view of human nature and experience.[2]

It would be difficult to quarrel with Becker's definition, given the wide range of his survey. His definition clearly requires modification, however, if it is to be applicable within narrower national and chronological limits, and such a modification is particularly important in American literary history, where realism is used to characterize an entire age. What I propose to do, then, is to use Becker's criteria of verisimilitude, representativeness, and objectivity as a means of approaching a definition of realism as it actually functioned in the late nineteenth-century American novel. My belief is that late nineteenth-century American realism varies from Becker's definition in two important ways. First, it achieves a greater diversity in subject matter than is suggested by the criterion of the representative. Secondly, it is essentially subjective and idealistic in its view of human nature and experience—that is, it is ethically idealistic. Three texts will illustrate my thesis: William Dean Howells's *The Rise of Silas Lapham* (1885), Mark Twain's *Adventures of Huckleberry Finn* (1884), and Henry James's *What Maisie Knew* (1897). I realize, of course, that earlier or later works by these novelists may or may not support my belief, and that works by other contemporaneous authors may contradict it as well. I am also aware that the realism of the nineties was in many respects less optimistic than that of the seventies. But the three works chosen are characteristic and well-known novels by the three leading realists of the period, and a generalization drawn from them need not be universally applicable to have implications for the period as a whole.

The three works are novels of manners in the sense that each focuses on the relationship of its central character to a particular social world. Each introduces a moral tension or conflict between the protagonist and his milieu. *The Rise of Silas Lapham* centers on the individual's relation to the business world; *Huck Finn* on his relation to the world of formalized codes of social belief and behavior; *What Maisie Knew* to the world of extramarital sexual intrigue.

The Rise of Silas Lapham clearly fulfills the initial two criteria of Becker's definition. Indeed, it is offered as a prime example of realistic fiction by Gordon Haight in his essay on Howells in the *Literary History of the United States* and by M. H. Abrams in his definition of realism in *A Glossary of Literary Terms*. The world of Silas Lapham is that of commonplace late nineteenth-century Boston. Here is no Ahab pursuing his whale with monomaniacal frenzy, no Leatherstocking matching wits and skill with red or white foes in the forest, no Chillingworth brewing potions, but Lapham going down to business each day, taking pride in his family, his trotter, his success in the world. That world, however, is not free from evil, and the moral drama in which Ahab, Leatherstocking, and Chillingworth played is still on the boards. But now, in everyday Boston, evil is more commonplace, is more that which we are accustomed to in our everyday affairs, is more realistic, if you will. It is the falsifications of Silas's former business partner; it is the willingness of the English agents to defraud their backers; it is Silas's own hardhearted treatment of his partner earlier in their careers. Moreover, evil is now so prevalent that the individual immersed in it is frequently unaware that he is participating in or committing evil. The point of the novel, however, is that Silas, though years of business life have partially atrophied his moral sense, does, at a moment of crisis, realize that a particular action is evil and does have the moral strength to make the correct choice. In his rejection of the opportunity to save his fortune, he rises not only above his earlier moral muteness, but also (and more importantly) above the society around him. He is ultimately morally superior to the business world which is his world.

Of course, Howells advocated probability of motive, and Silas's moral values do not appear from nowhere. They are founded in his poor but honest Vermont boyhood and in his wife's conscience. But explaining the source of an action does not make that action probable. Howells's belief in Silas's ability to rise above his world is basically idealistic, since it is a private belief in what should be rather than a depiction of what usually is. While Howells's conception of man and society is not crudely primitivistic, it owes much to a belief in the individual's innate moral sense and in the corrupting effects of the pressures of society. Such a belief does not have to be set in a jungle or forest to be operative.

Adventures of Huckleberry Finn, like much of Twain's work, is in the local color and tall tale traditions. From both of these Twain derived an emphasis on verisimilitude of detail. In *Huck Finn*, Twain's introductory note on accents is an indication of his conscious attempt to achieve accurate detail. But though Tom and Huck and Jim may be representative characters, their adventures are picaresque and are unusual rather than commonplace. We sometimes forget that the plot of the novel encompasses a full range of acts of violence, from the ambuscade of the Arabs to the near-lynching of Jim. It is possible, however, to struggle with the idea that the total effect of *Huck Finn* is realistic despite the extraordinary nature of Huck's adventures. This effect is partially gained by the satiric thrust of the novel, by its constant puncturing of the falsely heroic and the sentimental, by its burlesque of the extraordinary rather than its literal acceptance of it. In addition, *Huck Finn* is somewhat like *Tom Jones* in that the intense verisimilitude of detail in the portrayal of individual incidents and characters dominates the novel and tends to blur the exceptional quality of the incidents themselves. In short, part of Twain's purpose in his use of the extraordinary is to deflate it, and his use of vividly concrete detail helps achieve this end. In any case, though Twain does not completely fulfill the criterion of the representative, he nevertheless in his own way justifies his traditional inclusion among the realists.

In Huck Finn, as in *The Rise of Silas Lapham*, the social world is the embodiment of evil. Twain's world is larger than Howells's, however, and includes many forms of codified and institutionalized behavior and belief. Huck's decision not to inform on Jim (in the chapter "You Can't Pray a Lie") reveals the power of such codes. His resolution, Huck decides, is wrong and will result in his damnation. The irony, of course, is that he is led to this conclusion by what he knows is right—the code of slavery—although he does what he is instinctively led to do. Like Howells, then, Twain indicated that the world around us is frequently corrupt and false. This belief, which received its most obvious fictional representation in Huck's crisis, is also apparent in several other major incidents in the novel and in its very structure. Tom's romantic code of behavior, the code of the feud, of honor, of the mob, all are shown to lead to tragedy or near-tragedy—to the true damnation of the participant. Huck and Jim, drifting down the Mississippi, seek to evade these codes.

As Howells had done, Twain revealed his faith in man's ability to rise above the evil around him and achieve an ethical victory. Huck's moral values, like those of Silas, are effectively anticipated, since he has come to know and to value Jim as a companion in escape and as a human being. But

Huck's ability to make the correct moral choice despite the world around him is both more brilliantly ironic and more fundamentally idealistic than Silas's. Silas at least knew what was right and what was wrong. Huck must struggle against a false knowledge of right and wrong, and his correct decision is indicative of Twain's faith in the individual's ability to rise above society even when he is unaware that he is so doing.

What Maisie Knew is a psychological novel. James's interest, as he tells in his preface, was not primarily in the story, but rather in its refraction through the intelligence of a child. This technique would both illumine her mind and—because of her youth and freshness of vision—cast an ironic glow over the sordidness of the story. In order to achieve this end, James informs us, verisimilitude required that the child be a female rather than "a rude little boy." In addition, in order for the child to be the major source of moral insight, as well as "ironic center," she would have to be invested with "perceptions easily and almost infinitely quickened" and great "vivacity of intelligence," though not "in a manner too grossly to affront probability." James's intent was to present experience through a consciousness that had the ability to absorb and contemplate experience and ultimately the ability to draw moral deductions from that process. The need for such a consciousness, it is clear, encouraged the choice of an unusual central intelligence, one exceptional in perception and sensitivity, and therefore beyond the range of the representative. Yet though the intelligence itself is unusual, verisimilitude and probability are maintained as guides in the presentation of the refractor, and the total effect is that of psychological realism. In other words, James's practice of the psychological novel inherently encouraged a violation of one of the criteria of realism while at the same time he attempted to achieve the effect of realism.

As Twain does in *Huck Finn*, James juxtaposes a child and an evil world. The various adults who constitute Maisie's world shuttle her among themselves either to vex one another or to provide a screen for illicit relations. By the close of the novel Maisie knows two things. She has a knowledge of the world of adult promiscuity, jealousy, and desire. She has also, however, discovered her moral sense, partially under the guidance of Mrs. Wix, but (as becomes apparent when Mrs. Wix herself almost succumbs at the close) more as a reaction against the world around her. It is as if the irritation of that world had caused her moral sense to emerge and at last to assert itself in her refusal to remain with Sir Claude, whom she loves, under circumstances which she recognizes as both absolutely and pragmatically evil. Maisie, too, then, has risen above the world and has achieved an arduous moral victory. Huck's victory was difficult because it required him to subvert the dictates of knowledge and conscience. Silas's victory required the sacrifice of riches, Maisie's of love. But for all three victory can be and is gained.

Howells, Twain, and James indicate the ideal possibilities of action within particular social contexts, rather than the way most men act within these contexts. Those who are willing to struggle against the general current, and to be damned or to sacrifice wealth and love in the name of principle, have been and still are the exception, not the rule. The three writers, in short, dramatize a vision of experience in which individuals achieve that which is still a goal for mankind at large. This view of experience is, of course, a traditional one of much humanistic art, as well as a product of the more masculine side of nineteenth-century American romantic idealism—the side that does not minimize the strength of the forces tending to corrupt the spirit of man while it continues to affirm both the necessary and probable victory of the human spirit over these forces. The three writers gain much of their thematic power from their adherence to this view of experience. It is not a view, however, which fulfills the criterion of realism requiring an objective rather than a subjective or idealistic vision of human nature and experience.

Moreover, two of the three writers extend the subject matter of realism beyond the representative. Howells alone fulfills this criterion, and is a kind of mean in this respect, whereas Twain devotes much of his attention to the unusual in incident, James to the unusual in character. The significance of this extension is that Twain and James, rather than Howells, indicate the direction American fiction was to take. For although very few twentieth-century novelists have been concerned with the commonplace, many of our major writers have been occupied with what it is possible to call the horizontal and vertical extensions of realism—that is, the fiction of external violence and interior monologue.

Late nineteenth-century American realism was attacked in its own time for unidealized pictures of commonplace life, and for many years continued to be so characterized; in fact, however, it was neither unidealized nor—for the most part—commonplace. Rather, in its variation from these two criteria of a conventional definition of realism—that is, in its ethical idealism and in its exploration of richly diverse experience—it achieved both its vitality and its promise of future growth.

2

Late Nineteenth-Century
American Naturalism

MOST LITERARY CRITICS and historians who attempt definitions are aware of the dangers and advantages inherent in this enterprise. But few, I believe, recognize that many literary genres and modes have their barriers
of established terms and ideas to overcome or outflank. The
writer who seeks to define tragedy usually finds that his definition takes shape around such traditional guideposts as the
tragic hero, the tragic flaw, recognition and catharsis, and so
on. American naturalism, as a concept, has two such chan-
nelled approaches to its definition. The first is that since naturalism comes after realism, and since it seems to take literature in the same direction as realism, it is primarily an
"extension" or continuation of realism—only a little different. The second almost inevitable approach involves this
difference. The major distinction between realism and naturalism, most critics agree, is the particular philosophical orientation of the naturalists. A traditional and widely accepted
concept of American naturalism, therefore, is that it is essentially realism infused with a pessimistic determinism. Rich-

ard Chase argues that American naturalism is realism with a "necessitarian ideology," and George J. Becker (defining all naturalism, including American) considers it as "no more than an emphatic and explicit philosophical position taken by some realists," the position being a "pessimistic materialistic determinism."[1] The common belief is that the naturalists were like the realists in their fidelity to the details of contemporary life, but that they depicted everyday life with a greater sense of the role of such causal forces as heredity and environment in determining behavior and belief.

This traditional approach to naturalism through realism and through philosophical determinism is historically justifiable and has served a useful purpose, but it has also handicapped thinking both about the movement as a whole and about individual works within the movement. It has resulted in much condescension toward those writers who are supposed to be naturalists yet whose fictional sensationalism (an aspect of romanticism) and moral ambiguity (a quality inconsistent with the absolutes of determinism) appear to make their work flawed specimens of the mode.

I would like, therefore, to propose a modified definition of late nineteenth-century American naturalism.[2] For the time being, let this be a working definition, to be amplified and made more concrete by the illustrations from which it has been drawn. I suggest that the naturalistic novel usually contains two tensions or contradictions, and that the two in conjunction comprise both an interpretation of experience and a particular aesthetic recreation of experience. In other words, the two constitute the theme and form of the naturalistic novel. The first tension is that between the subject matter of the naturalistic novel and the concept of man which emerges from this subject matter. The naturalist populates his novel primarily from the lower middle class or the lower class. His characters are the poor, the uneducated, the unsophisticated. His fictional world is that of the commonplace and unheroic in which life would seem to be chiefly the dull round of daily existence, as we ourselves usually conceive of our lives. But the naturalist discovers in this world those qualities of man usually associated with the heroic or adventurous, such as acts of violence and passion which involve sexual adventure or bodily strength and which culminate in desperate moments and violent death. A naturalistic novel is thus an extension of realism only in the sense that both modes often deal with the local and contemporary. The naturalist, however, discovers in this material the extraordinary and excessive in human nature.

The second tension involves the theme of the naturalistic novel. The naturalist often describes his characters as though they are conditioned and controlled by environment, heredity, instinct, or chance. But he also suggests a compensating humanistic value in his characters or their fates which affirms the significance of the individual and of his life. The tension here is that between the naturalist's desire to represent in fiction the new, discomforting truths which he has found in the ideas and life of his late nineteenth-century world, and also his desire to find some meaning in experience which reasserts the validity of the human enterprise. The naturalist appears to say that although the individual may be a cipher in a world made amoral by man's lack of responsibility for his fate, the imagination refuses to accept this formula as the total meaning of life and so seeks a new basis for man's sense of his own dignity and importance.

The naturalistic novel is therefore not so superficial or reductive as it implicitly appears to be in its conventional definition. It involves a belief that life on its lowest levels is not so simple as it seems to be from higher levels. It suggests that even the least significant human being can feel and strive powerfully and can suffer the extraordinary consequences of his emotions, and that no range of human experience is free of the moral complexities and ambiguities which Milton set his fallen angels to debating.[3] Naturalism reflects an affirmative ethical conception of life, for it asserts the value of all life by endowing the lowest character with emotion and defeat and with moral ambiguity, no matter how poor or ignoble he may seem. The naturalistic novel derives much of its aesthetic effect from these contrasts. It involves us in the experience of a life both commonplace and extraordinary, both familiar and strange, both simple and complex. It pleases us with its sensationalism without affronting our sense of probability. It discovers the "romance of the commonplace," as Frank Norris put it. Thus, the melodramatic sensationalism and moral "confusion" which are often attacked in the naturalistic novel should really be incorporated into a normative definition of the mode and be recognized as its essential constituents.

The three novels which I have chosen to illustrate this definition, and also to suggest the possible range of variation within it, are Frank Norris's *McTeague* (1899), Theodore Dreiser's *Sister Carrie* (1900), and Stephen Crane's *The Red Badge of Courage* (1895). These works are important novels by the three leading late nineteenth-century American naturalists, and each novel has frequently been read as a key example of its author's values and his fictional form. A definition drawn from these three novels will not be applicable to all late nineteenth-century naturalistic fiction. But, given the significance of these writers and of these novels, it would, I believe, be a useful introduction to this major movement in American literary history.

A good deal of *McTeague* is devoted to depicting the routine, ordered world of Polk Street, the lower middle class service street in San Francisco on which McTeague practices and lives. The life of Polk Street enters the novel in two ways—through set pieces describing street activities or the daily lives of the central characters in relation to the life of the street, and through constant incidental allusion to its activities and inhabitants. Norris dramatically establishes Polk Street as above all a life of the repetitious and constant. The street exists as a source of the ordered and the routine in McTeague's life, as a world where the harness shop, the grocery, and the car conductors' coffee joint are always available in their set roles, where the children go to school at the same time each day, followed by the shop clerks coming to work, and so on. McTeague is settled and content in this life, and we recognize that his inner needs and outer world are in harmony.

A central theme in Norris's work is that beneath the surface of our placid, everyday lives there is turbulence, that the romance of the extraordinary is not limited to the distant in time and place but can be found "in the brownstone house on the corner and in the office building downtown."[4] Norris therefore used the incident which had stimulated him to write the novel, a vicious murder in a San Francisco kindergarten, as a controlling paradox in *McTeague* as in scene after scene he introduces the sensational into the commonplace activities and setting of Polk Street. So we have such incidents as McTeague grossly kissing the anesthetized Trina in his dental parlor, or the nearly murderous fight between Marcus and McTeague at the picnic. Some of the best moments in the novel powerfully unite these two streams of the commonplace and the extraordinary. In one such moment the frightened and incoherent Trina, having just found Maria's corpse with its cut throat and its blood soaked clothes, rushes out into the everyday routine of Polk Street and has difficulty convincing the butcher's boy that something is wrong or even convincing herself that it is not improper "to make a disturbance and create a scene in the street."[5]

Norris believed that the source of this violence beneath the surface placidity of life is the presence in all men of animal qualities which have played a major role in man's evolutionary development but which are now frequently atavistic and destructive.[6] Norris's theme is that man's racial atavism (particularly his brute sexual desires) and man's individual family heritage (alcoholic degeneracy in McTeague's case) can combine as a force toward reversion, toward a return to the emotions and instincts of man's animal past. McTeague is in one sense a "special case" of reversion, since his atavistic brutality is in part caused by his degenerate parents. He is also, however, any man caught up in the net of sex, and in this second aspect of man's inherited animal nature Norris introduces a tragic element into McTeague's fall, an element which contributes to the novel's thematic tension.

In describing the courtship of Trina and McTeague, Norris is at pains to stress their overt sexual innocence yet intuitive sexuality. The woman in Trina "was not yet awakened; she was yet, as one might say, without sex" (14). For McTeague, Trina is his "first experience. With her the feminine element suddenly entered his little world. It was not only her that he saw and felt, it was the woman, the whole sex, an entire new humanity" (16). Despite their innocence and lack of experience, both react intuitively and atavistically—McTeague desiring to seize and possess her, she instinctively withdrawing yet desiring to be conquered.

The most important sexual encounter between McTeague and Trina occurs at the B Street Station where McTeague for a second time proposes. When Trina hesitates, he seizes her "in his enormous arms, crushing down her struggle with his immense strength. Then Trina gave up, all in an instant, turning her head to his. They kissed each other, grossly, full in the mouth" (48). Within the literary conventions of the day, this kiss symbolizes Trina's sexual submission. At this moment the strands in the web of sexual determinism begin to pull taut, for "the instant she allowed him to kiss her, he thought less of her. She was not so desirable, after all" (48). McTeague senses this diminution along with a dim awareness "that this must be so, that it belonged to the changeless order of things—the man desiring the woman only for what she withholds; the woman worshipping the man for that which she yields up to him. With each concession gained the man's desire cools; with every surrender made the woman's adoration increases" (48). Norris is concerned in this second meeting not with a special flaw in McTeague or Trina but with a sexual determinism affecting all men. The possessive sexual desire of the man aroused by the first woman he experiences sensually, the instinctive desire of the woman for sexual submission responding to the first man who assaults her—these are the atavistic animal forces which bring Trina and McTeague together.

A major theme in *McTeague* is therefore that of the sexual tragedy of man and woman. Caught up by drives and instincts beyond their control or comprehension, they mate by chance. In *McTeague* sex is that which comes to all men and women, disrupting their lives and placing them in relationships which the sanctity of marriage cannot prevent from ending in chaos and destruction. Norris does not tell the old tale of the fallen fornicator, as he does in *Vandover and the Brute*, but rather reaches out toward the unexplored ground of the human dilemma of sexual attraction.

The tension between this deterministic aspect of *McTeague* and its humanistic element does not lie in McTeague as a fully developed tragic figure. Rather, it is contained in the theme that man can seldom escape the violence inherent in his own nature, that man's attempt to achieve an ordered world is constantly thwarted by man himself. Norris devotes much attention to the element of order in the details of McTeague's life not only because of his belief in the romance of the commonplace but because the destruction of that order is the source of the tragic quality in McTeague's fall and of our own compassionate involvement with him despite his grotesqueness. Norris carefully documents McTeague's life as a dentist and as an inhabitant of Polk Street because the habitual tasks and minor successes of this life represent the order and stability which McTeague requires. In the course of the novel we begin to feel compassion for him as he becomes a victim of Trina's avarice and as we recognize that his emerging brutality is at least partly the result of the destruction of his world. When McTeague learns that he can no longer practice dentistry, his reaction is that of a man whose life is emptied of all meaning. In a scene of considerable power Trina comes upon him sitting in his dental chair, "looking stupidly out of the windows, across the roofs opposite, with an unseeing gaze, his red hands lying idly in his lap" (151). We are never completely one with McTeague; his brute strength and dull mind put us off. But because he is trapped in the universal net of sex, and because we recognize the poignancy of the loss of his world, we respond to him ultimately as a human being in distress, as a figure of some significance despite his limitations—as a man, in short, whose fall contains elements of the tragic.

For *McTeague* is in part a tragic novel. True, McTeague neither bears full responsibility for his fate nor is he in any sense noble or profound. He is rather like Gervaise in *L'Assommoir*: they are both poor creatures who want above all a place to rest and be content, yet who are brought low by their needs and desires. There is a sense of common humanity in McTeague's fall, and that quality is perhaps the modern residue of the tragic theme, since we are no longer certain of man's transcendent nobility or of the reality of major responsibility for our fates. The theme of *McTeague* is not that drunkenness leads to a tragic fall, but that tragedy is inherent in the human situation given man's animal past and the possibility that he will be dominated by that past in particular circumstances. Norris does not deny the strength of man's past or present animality, but neither does he deny the poignancy of the fall of even such a gross symbol of this animality as McTeague. It is out of this tension that much of the meaning and power of the novel arises.

Even more than Norris, Theodore Dreiser creates a sense of the solidity of life. His early novels in particular affirm that we cannot escape the impact of physical reality and that this fact is one of the few that man may know with certainty. So the several worlds of Carrie—her sister's working class existence, her life with Drouet in Chicago and with Hurstwood in New York—achieve a sense of massiveness both in their painstaking documentation and in their inescapable effect on Carrie. The effect on us, however, is not only to enforce a sense of the importance of clothes, of furniture, of how much one owes the grocer and of exactly how much one earns and spends—the impact, too, is of normalcy, of the steady pace of life, since life does indeed seem to be measured out in coffee spoons. Dreiser's ability to capture the tangible commonplace of everyday existence powerfully suggests that the commonplace and everyday are the essence of experience, particularly since he returns again and again to the unexciting details of the furnishings of an apartment or the contents of a meal. Moreover, Dreiser's dispassionate tone contributes to this effect. This is not to say that his fiction lacks an ironic dimension. He frequently sets events or beliefs in ironic juxtaposition, as when Carrie is worried that Hurstwood will discover that she and Drouet are unmarried though she herself is unaware that Hurstwood is married. But Dreiser's irony differs from Crane's intense and pervasive ironic vision of life, a vision which colors every incident or observation in Crane's work with the implication that things are not what they seem. Dreiser's plodding, graceless paragraphs imply the opposite—that the concrete world he so seriously details is real and discernible and that nothing can shake or undermine it.

Dreiser's central theme in *Sister Carrie*, however, sets forth the idea—Lionel Trilling to the contrary[7]—that the physically real is not the only reality and that men seek something in life beyond it. His theme is that those of a finer, more intense, more emotional nature who desire to break out of their normal solid world—whether it be a Carrie oppressed by the dull repetitiousness and crudity of her sister's home, or a Hurstwood jaded by the middle class trivialities of his family—that when such as these strive to discover a life approximate to their natures they introduce into their lives the violent and the extraordinary. Carrie leaves her sister's flat for two illicit alliances, attracted to each man principally by the opportunities he offers for a better life. Drouet and Hurstwood represent to her not so much wealth or sexual attraction as an appeal to something intangibly richer and fuller in herself. She is drawn to each in turn, and then finally to Ames, because each appeals to some quality in her temperament which she finds unfulfilled in her life of the moment. Dreiser's depiction

of her almost asexual relations with all of these men represents less his capitulation to contemporary publishing restric-
tions (although some of this is present) than his desire that the
three characters reflect the upward course of Carrie's discovery and realization of her inner nature. Finally, Carrie's career on the stage symbolizes both the emotional intensity she
is capable of bringing to life and the fact that she requires the
intrinsically extraordinary and exciting world of the theatre
to call forth and embody her emotional depth.

Hurstwood also introduces the sensational into his life by
reaching out beyond his established world. For him, the extraordinary arises from his attempt to gain and then hold
Carrie, since she represents to him his last opportunity to
grasp life fully and intensely. We follow him as he breaks the
seemingly set mold of his life by his theft and by his elope-
ment. His participation in the violence of the street car strike
is his final attempt to recover his fortunes (and Carrie) in
New York. With Carrie gone, he sinks still further and eventually commits suicide.

Hurstwood's suicide can be explored as a typical example
of Dreiser's combination of the concretely commonplace and
the sensational. It takes place in a cheap Bowery hotel.
Hurstwood's method is to turn on the gas, not resolutely but
hesitantly, and then to say weakly, "What's the use?" as he
"stretched himself to rest."[8] Dreiser thus submerges an inherently sensational event in the trivial and unemotional. He
not only "takes the edge off" the extraordinariness of the
event by his full and detached elaboration of its commonplace setting but also casts it in the imagery of enervation and
rest. This scene is in one sense a special instance, since
Hurstwood seeks death as a refuge. But Dreiser's total effect
as a novelist is often similar to the effect produced by this
scene as he dramatizes throughout *Sister Carrie* the solidity

and therefore seeming normalcy of experience and yet its underlying extraordinariness if man seeks beyond the routine. His principal aesthetic impact, however, is different from that of Norris, who appears to combine the sensational and commonplace much as Dreiser does. Norris's effect is basically that of dramatic sensationalism, of the excitement of violence and sudden death. Dreiser's effect is more thematic and less scenic because he colors the sensational with the same emotional stolidity with which he characterizes all experience. It is not only that the sensational and extraordinary exist in our commonplace lives, Dreiser appears to say, but that they are so pervasive and implicit in our experience that their very texture differs little from the ordinary course of events. Thus, such potentially exciting and dramatically sensational moments in Dreiser's fiction as the seduction of Jennie Gerhardt or the imprisonment of Frank Cowperwood have an almost listless dullness compared to Norris's treatment of parallel events in his fiction.

Carrie, like many of Dreiser's characters, has her life shaped by chance and need. Chance involves her with Drouet and later plays a large role in Hurstwood's theft and therefore in her own departure with him. Her needs are of two kinds—first to attain the tangible objects and social symbols of comfort and beauty which she sees all around her in Chicago and New York, and then to be loved. Of the major forces in her life, it is primarily her desire for objects that furnish a sense of physical and mental well-being—for fine clothing and furniture and attractive apartments and satisfactory food—which determines much of her life. As she gains more of these, her fear of returning to poverty and crudity—to her sister's condition—impels her to seek even more vigorously. Much of the concrete world that Dreiser fills in so exhaustively in *Sister Carrie* thus exists as a determining force in Carrie's life, first moving her to escape it, as in her encounters with working-class Chicago, and then to reach out for it, as when Drouet takes her to a good restaurant and buys her some fashionable clothes and so introduces into her imagination the possibility of making these a part of her life.

But Carrie's response to her needs is only one side of her nature. She also possesses a quality which is intrinsic to her being, though its external shape (a Drouet, a dress seen on the street) is determined by accidental circumstance. For in this his first novel Dreiser endows Carrie with the same capacity to wonder and to dream which he felt so strongly in himself. It is this ability to dream about the nature of oneself and one's fate and of where one is going and how one will get there and to wonder whether happiness is real and possible or only an illusion—it is this capacity which ultimately questions the reality and meaning of the seemingly solid and plain world in which we find ourselves.

This "dream" quality underlies the most striking symbol in the novel, the rocking chair. The rocking chair has correctly been interpreted as principally a symbol of circularity because Carrie rocks on her first night in Chicago and again at the novel's close in her New York apartment.[9] Dreiser seems to imply by the symbol that nothing really has happened to Carrie, that although her outer circumstances have changed, she is essentially the same both morally and spiritually. The symbol does indeed function in this way, but it also, in its persistence, reflects Carrie's continuing ability to wonder about herself and her future and this reveals that her imaginative response to life has not been dulled by experience. Although she has not achieved the happiness that she thought accompanied the life she desired and which she now has, she will continue to search. Perhaps Ames represents the next, higher step in this quest, Dreiser implies. But in any case, she possesses this inner force, a force which is essentially bold and free. Although it brings her worry and loneliness—the rocking chair symbolizes these as well—it is an element in her which Dreiser finds estimable and moving. She will always be the dreamer, Dreiser says, and though her dreams take an earthly shape controlled by her world, and though she is judged immoral by the world because she violates its conventions in pursuit of her dreams, she has for Dreiser—and for us, I believe—meaning and significance and stature because of her capacity to rock and dream, to question life and to pursue it. Thus Carrie seeks to fulfill each new venture and gain each new object as though these were the only realities of life, and yet by her very dissatisfaction and questioning of what she has gained to imply the greater reality of the mind and spirit that dreams and wonders. The rocking chair goes nowhere, but it moves, and in that paradox lies Dreiser's involvement with Carrie and his ability to communicate the intensity and nature of her quest. For in his mind, too, the world is both solid and unknowable, and man is ever pursuing and never finding.

The Red Badge of Courage also embodies a different combination of the sensational and commonplace than that found in *McTeague*. Whereas Norris demonstrates that the violent and the extraordinary are present in seemingly dull and commonplace lives, Crane, even more than Dreiser, is intent on revealing the commonplace nature of the seemingly exceptional. In *The Red Badge* Henry Fleming is a raw, untried country youth who seeks the romance and glory of war but who finds that his romantic, chivalric preconceptions of battle are false. Soldiers and generals do not strike heroic poses;

the dead are not borne home triumphantly on their shields but fester where they have fallen; and courage is not a conscious striving for an ideal mode of behavior but a temporary delirium derived from animal fury and social pride or fear. A wounded officer worries about the cleanliness of his uniform; a soldier sweats and labors at his arms "like a laborer in a foundry";[10] and mere chance determines rewards and punishments—the death of a Conklin, the red badge of a Fleming. War to Crane is like life itself in its injustice, in its mixing of the ludicrous and the momentarily exhilarating, in its self-deceptions, and in its acceptance of appearances for realities. Much of Crane's imagery in the novel is therefore consciously and pointedly antiheroic, not only in his obviously satirical use of conventional chivalric imagery in unheroic situations (a soldier bearing a rumor comes "waving his [shirt] banner-like" and adopting "the important air of a herald in red and gold" [5]) but also more subtly in his use of machine and animal imagery to deflate potentially heroic moments.

Crane's desire to devalue the heroic in war stems in part from his stance as an ironist reacting against a literary and cultural tradition of idealized courage and chivalry. But another major element in his desire to reduce war to the commonplace arises from his casting of Fleming's experiences in the form of a "life" or initiation allegory. Henry Fleming is the universal youth who leaves home unaware of himself or the world. His participation in battle is his introduction to life as for the first time he tests himself and his preconceptions of experience against experience itself. He emerges at the end of the battle not entirely self-perceptive or firm-willed—Crane is too much the ironist for such a reversal—but rather as one who has encountered some of the strengths and some of the failings of himself and others. Crane implies that although

Fleming may again run from battle and although he will no doubt always have the human capacity to rationalize his weaknesses, he is at least no longer the innocent.

If *The Red Badge* is viewed in this way—that is, as an anti-heroic allegory of "life"—it becomes clear that Crane is representing in his own fashion the naturalistic belief in the interpenetration of the commonplace and the sensational. All life, Crane appears to be saying, is a struggle, a constant sea of violence in which we inevitably immerse ourselves and in which we test our beliefs and our values. War is an appropriate allegorical symbol of this test, for to Crane violence is the very essence of life, not in the broad Darwinian sense of a struggle for existence or the survival of the fittest, but rather in the sense that the proving and testing of oneself, conceived both realistically and symbolically, entails the violent and the deeply emotional, that the finding of oneself occurs best in moments of stress and is itself often an act of violence. To Crane, therefore, war as an allegorical setting for the emergence of youth into knowledge embodies both the violence of this birth and the commonplaces of life which the birth reveals—that men are controlled by the trivial, the accidental, the degradingly unheroic, despite the preservation of such accoutrements of the noble as a red badge or a captured flag. Crane shows us what Norris and Dreiser only suggest, that there is no separation between the sensational and the commonplace, that the two are coexistent in every aspect and range of life. He differs from Norris in kind and from Dreiser in degree in that his essentially ironic imagination leads him to reverse the expected and to find the commonplace in the violent rather than the sensational beneath the trivial. His image of life as an unheroic battle captures in one ironic symbol both his romanticism and his naturalism—or, in less literary terms, his belief that we reveal character in violence but that human character is predominantly fallible and self-deceptive.

Much of Crane's best fiction displays this technique of ironic deflation. In *Maggie*, a young urchin defends the honor of Rum Alley on a heap of gravel; in "The Open Boat," the stalwart oiler suffers an inconsequential and meaningless death; in "The Blue Hotel," the death of the Swede is accompanied by a derisive sign on the cash register; and in "The Bride Comes to Yellow Sky," the long-awaited "chivalric" encounter is thwarted by the bride's appearance. Each of these crucial or significant events has at its core Crane's desire to reduce the violent and extraordinary to the commonplace, a reduction which indicates both his ironic vision of man's romantic pretensions and his belief in the reality of the fusion of the violent and the commonplace in experience.

As was true of Norris and Dreiser, Crane's particular way of combining the sensational and the commonplace is closely related to the second major aspect of his naturalism, the thematic tension or complexity he embodies in his work. *The Red Badge* presents a vision of a man as a creature capable of advancing in some areas of knowledge and power but forever imprisoned within the walls of certain inescapable human and social imitations. Crane depicts the similarity between Henry Fleming's "will" and an animal's instinctive response to crisis or danger. He also presents Fleming's discovery that he is enclosed in a "moving box" of "tradition and law" (21) even at those moments when he believes himself capable of rational decision and action—that the opinions and actions of other men control and direct him. Lastly, Crane dramatizes Fleming's realization that although he can project his emotions into natural phenomena and therefore derive comfort from a sense of nature's identification with his desires and needs, nature and man are really two, not one, and nature offers no reliable or useful guide to experience or to action. But, despite Crane's perception of these limitations and inadequacies, he does not paint a totally bleak picture of man in *The Red Badge*. True, Fleming's own sanguine view of himself at the close of the novel—that he is a man—cannot be taken at face value. Fleming's self-evaluations contrast ironically with his motives and actions throughout the novel, and his final estimation of himself represents primarily man's ability to be proud of his public deeds while rationalizing his private failings.

But something has happened to Fleming which Crane values and applauds. Early in the novel Fleming feels at odds with his comrades. He is separated from them by doubts about his behavior under fire and by fear of their knowledge of his doubts. These doubts and fears isolate him from his fellows, and his isolation is intensified by his growing awareness that the repressive power of the "moving box" of his regiment binds him to a group from which he now wishes to escape. Once in battle, however, Fleming becomes "not a man but a member" as he is "welded into a common personality which was dominated by a single desire" (30). The "subtle battle brotherhood" (31) replaces his earlier isolation, and in one sense the rest of the novel is devoted to Fleming's loss and recovery of his feeling of oneness with his fellows. After his initial success in battle, Henry loses this quality as he deserts his comrades and then wanders away from his regiment in actuality and in spirit. His extreme stage of isolation from the regiment and from mankind occurs when he abandons the tattered soldier. After gaining a "red badge" which symbolically reunites him with those soldiers who remained and fought, he returns to his regiment and participates successfully in the last stages of the battle. Here, as everywhere in Crane, there is a deflating irony, for Henry's "red badge" is not a true battle wound. But despite the tainted origin of this symbol of fraternity, its effect on Henry and his fellows is real and significant. He is accepted gladly when he returns, and in his renewed confidence and pride he finds strength and a kind of joy. Crane believed that this feeling of trust and mutual confidence among men is essential, and it is one of the few values he confirms again and again in his fiction. It is this quality which knits together the four men in the open boat and lends them moral strength. And it is the absence of this quality and its replacement by fear and distrust which characterizes the world of "The Blue Hotel" and causes the tragic denouement in that story.

Crane thus points out that courage has primarily a social reality, that it is a quality which exists not absolutely but by virtue of other men's opinions, and that the social unity born of a courageous fellowship may therefore be based on self-deception or on deception of others. He also demonstrates that this bond of fellowship may be destructive and oppressive when it restricts or determines individual choice, as in the "moving box" of the regiment. Fleming, after all, at first stands fast because he is afraid of what his comrades will do or think, and then runs because he feels that the rest of the regiment is deserting as well. But Crane also maintains that in social cohesion man gains both what little power of self-preservation he possesses and a gratifying and necessary sense of acceptance and acknowledgement difficult to attain otherwise. Crane therefore establishes a vital organic relationship between his deflation of the traditional idea of courage and his assertion of the need for and the benefits of social unity. He attacks the conventional heroic ideal by showing that a man's actions in battle are usually determined by his imitation of the actions of others—by the group as a whole. But this presentation of the reality and power of the group also suggests the advantages possible in group unity and group action.

There is, then, a moral ambiguity in Crane's conception of man's relationship with his fellows, an ambiguity which permeates his entire vision of man. Henry Fleming falsely acquires a symbol of group identity, yet this symbol aids him in recovering his group identity and in benefiting the group. Man's involvement with others forces him into psychic compulsion (Henry's running away), yet this involvement is the source of his sense of psychic oneness. Henry is still for the most part self-deceived at the close of the novel, but if he is not the "man" he thinks he has become, he has at least shed some of the innocence of the child. Crane's allegory of life as a battle is thus appropriate for another reason besides its relevance to the violence of discovery. Few battles are clearly or cleanly won or lost, and few soldiers are clearly God's chosen. But men struggle, and in their struggle they learn something about their limitations and capacities and something about the nature of their relations with their fellow men, and this knowledge is rewarding even though they never discover the full significance or direction of the campaign in which they are engaged.

The primary goal of the late nineteenth-century American naturalists was not to demonstrate the overwhelming and oppressive reality of the material forces present in our lives. Their attempt, rather, was to represent the intermingling in life of controlling force and individual worth. If they were not always clear in distinguishing between these two qualities in experience, it was partly because they were novelists responding to life's complexities and were not philosophers categorizing experience, and partly because they were sufficiently of our own time to doubt the validity of moral or any other absolutes. The naturalists do not dehumanize man. They rather suggest new or modified areas of value in man while engaged in destroying such old and to them unreal sources of human self-importance as romantic love or moral responsibility or heroism. They are some distance from traditional Christian humanism, but they have not yet reached the despairing emptiness of Joseph Wood Krutch's *The Modern Temper*. One should not deny the bleak view of man inherent in McTeague's or Hurstwood's decline or in Fleming's self-deceptions, but neither should one forget that to the naturalists man's weaknesses and limited knowledge and thwarted desires were still sources of compassion and worth as well as aspects of the human condition to be more forthrightly acknowledged than writers had done in the past.

Nor is naturalism simply a piling on of unselective blocks of documentation. A successful naturalistic novel is like any successful work of art in that it embodies a cogent relationship between its form (its particular combination of the commonplace and sensational) and its theme (its particular tension between the individually significant and the deterministic). There is a major difference, within general similarities, between Norris's discovery of the sensational in the commonplace and Crane's dramatization of the triviality of the sensational. This variation derives principally from the differing thematic tension in the two novels. Norris wishes to demonstrate the tragic destruction of McTeague's commonplace world by the violence inherent in all life, whereas Crane wishes to dramatize Fleming's violent initiation into the commonplace nature of the heroic. Norris and Crane occupy positions in American naturalism analogous to that of Wordsworth and Byron in English romanticism. Like the poetry of the two earlier figures, their fiction expresses strikingly individual and contrasting visions of experience, yet does so within a body of shared intellectual and literary assumptions belonging to their common historical and literary moment. The naturalistic novel is thus no different from any other major literary genre in its complex intermingling of form and theme, in its reflection of an author's individual temperament and experience within large generic similarities, and—at its best—in its thematic depth and importance. We have done a disservice to the late nineteenth-century American naturalists by our earlier simplistic conception of their art.

3

Nineteenth-Century American Naturalism: An Approach Through Form

MOST CRITICS WHO discuss American literary naturalism do so both warily and wearily. What is one to say about this significant yet intellectually disreputable body of literature which ranges from the stylism of Crane to the anti-stylism of Dreiser, which is often characterized by a species of adolescent awe at the fact that the human will is circumscribed, and which, with the exception of Dreiser, continues into modern American literature more as a long shadow than as a living presence? After one has noted the foreign influences, the documentation of sensational lower class life, the too-ready absorption of contemporary scientism, and the intellectual confusion, there seems little to say, except perhaps to speculate on the twist of literary fortune which casts up this sport on the American scene while for the most part sparing our English cousins.

Edwin Cady's essay "Three Sensibilities: Romancer, Realist, Naturalist," in his *The Light of Common Day* (1971), is typical of much discussion of American naturalism. In order to distinguish among the major nineteenth-century American literary movements, Cady adopts the strategy of defining the literary sensibility or temperament which produced a characteristic work within each movement. He is remarkably perceptive and persuasive in describing the sensibilities of the romancer and the realist—the quality of mind which seeks to transcend the limitations of experience in the one and to affirm the moral and aesthetic value of our limited but shared perception and experience in the other—but his strategy fails him when he reaches naturalism. At this point he throws up his hands in despair at the incongruity between what naturalists appeared to believe about human nature and what such a belief implies about their sensibilities. He therefore concludes that in fact there is no such thing as a naturalist sensibility; there are only covert humanists and ameliorists playing with naturalistic ideas and subject matter. "Upon Norris and all the other artists of his richly endowed generation," Cady writes, "the sensibility of the naturalist exerted a magnetic pull. Nobody was a naturalist. There really are no naturalists in American literature. Everybody born after the Civil War felt and responded after his fashion to the terrible pull of a sensibility in the grounds for which nobody finally believed."[1]

Cady's observation is of course true, but its truth is for the most part critically unproductive. Almost every major writer in any age is a humanist, and in more or less degree the distinctive shape he gives his qualified endorsement of the human condition is a literary mask—be it romanticist, realist, or naturalist—through which a gifted and feeling man speaks. To say that there are no true naturalists but only the "magnetic pull" of a contemporaneously compelling literary mask is to state an extreme instance of a general truth. Moreover, like so many critics of American naturalism, Cady begins with an ideal construct of the naturalistic ethos—principally that of a universe of forces in which man is an insignificant and even contemptible figure—and then finds that few naturalists coherently or consistently inform their work with this ethos. Thus, he approaches naturalism with the almost instinctive distaste of the intellectual toward writers who handle ideas sloppily.

What, then, are we to do with American naturalism, since it seems intractable to criticism and since we cannot erase it from our literary history? A possible way out of our dilemma is to seek critical approaches or strategies which bypass the hazards which result from considering naturalism primarily as a movement closely allied to its contemporary intellectual and social background. We might posit, for example, a critic of naturalism who has read a great many novels from Defoe to the recent past but little else. This reader would have a kind of sophisticated innocence. He would possess much awareness of how fiction works as an art form and of major changes in the form of the novel throughout its history, but he would be unaware of all matters involving the origins and the ideological and cultural context of particular moments in the history of the form. From the vantage point of this sophisticated innocence, our critic could look at some characteristic late nineteenth-century American novels to determine if they share, not traces of evolutionary thought or Zolaesque sensationalism, but rather a distinctive fictional style or shape which can be interpreted as the response of this generation of writers to their experience and which distinguishes this moment from other moments.

To begin, then. From the angle of vision of a sophisticated innocence, a work of fiction takes its form from its narrative of what happens to people when they interact with each other, or within themselves, or with their worlds, and thus create physical or psychological events. The major tradition in English and American fiction until the closing decades of the nineteenth century was to depict most sequences of events— that is, the physical, intellectual, or spiritual movement of characters through time—as progressive. Narratives were progressive not merely in the superficial sense of the moral romance, in which good characters were rewarded and evil ones punished, but also in the deeper sense of most great fiction from *Tom Jones* and *Pamela* to *The Scarlet Letter* and *Middlemarch*. Tom wins his Sophia and Pamela her Mr. B., the scarlet letter at last does its office, and Dorothea and Ladislaw though not as fresh as they once were are also not as illusioned. The world, in short, may be a difficult place, and man is imperfect, but the passage of time profits the bold and good hearted and leavens life with judgment if not with wisdom. The major characteristic of the form of the naturalistic novel is that it no longer reflects this certainty about the value of experience but rather expresses a profound doubt or perplexity about what happens in the course of time.

When I say "the form of a naturalistic novel," I mean, of course, not a single, describable entity but a complex of devices and techniques which differs in degree and kind from writer to writer and from novel to novel while still sharing certain general and therefore abstractable tendencies. In a book length study, I would attempt to discuss all of the more prominent of these narrative tendencies. But on this occasion, I can examine only one—the naturalistic symbol— though I hope that it is a choice which usefully illustrates my principal observation about the form of the naturalistic novel.[2]

Here, then, are three late nineteenth-century narratives that a reader bred on earlier fiction would expect to end with an effect of progressive development or change: a story in which an honest workingclass man begins to move into the lower middle class because of his occupation and because of an advantageous marriage; one in which a girl from the provinces survives the storms and hazards of the city and gains great success because of her natural abilities; and a third in which a raw country youth takes part in a great battle and proves his courage both to himself and to his comrades. In each of these novels—*McTeague, Sister Carrie,* and *The Red Badge of Courage*—there is a pervasive and striking symbol which, in a sense, accompanies the protagonist on his adventures. McTeague's is that of gold—the gold he works with as a dentist, the gold of Trina's hoard that he later covets, the gold mine that he discovers late in the novel, and in particular the gold tooth advertising sign which to him means success and prominence in his profession and therefore a confirmation of his shaky sense of personal and social sufficiency. Carrie's symbol is that of the rocking chair in which she so often sits and muses about the happiness that she longs for, whether her anticipated happiness be that of pleasure, success, or beauty. And Henry Fleming's is a wound, a red badge of courage which testifies to his fellows that he is not the coward he fears he may be.

A major characteristic of each of these symbols is that it functions ironically within the structure of its novel. McTeague acquires more and more gold, from his initial small dental supply to the gold tooth to Trina's gold coins to an entire mine. Yet despite his gain of this symbol of wealth and therefore presumably of class and esteem, his movement from midway in the novel is downward both socially and personally until he reaches his final condition of a pursued animal. Carrie looks out over the teeming streets on her first night in Chicago and rocks and dreams of a happiness which consists of smart clothes, flashy men, and evenings at the vaudeville theatre. Eight years later, at the close of the novel, she is a famous New York musical comedy actress and has acquired all of these and more but she still rocks and dreams of a happiness which might be hers if only she could devote herself to the art of dramatic expression. And Fleming, having run from the battlefield in terror, acquires his red badge by a blow from one of his own retreating comrades. But when his red badge of ignominy is divorced from its source, it quickly begins to act upon others and eventually upon Henry as a sign of his honorable participation in battle.

I do not wish to suggest that these symbols and the narratives in which they occur are entirely similar. Obviously, there is much difference in tone, in depth of implication, and in literary success between Norris' arbitrary and often fulsome gold symbolism, Dreiser's skillful and evocative use of the rocking chair as a rhythmic symbol in several senses, and Crane's reliance on an intense verbal as well as structural irony when describing the effects of Henry's wound. Yet the symbols perform parallel roles in their respective narratives in that they structure and inform our sense not only that human beings are flawed and ineffectual but also that experience itself does not guide, instruct, or judge human nature. One of the principal corollaries of a progressive view of time is the belief that man has the capacity to interact meaningfully with his world and to benefit from this interaction. But the effect of the naturalistic novel, as is suggested by its symbolic structure, is to reverse or heavily qualify this expectation. McTeague, Carrie, and Fleming are in a sense motionless in time. They have moved through experience but still only dimly comprehend it and themselves, and thus their journeys through time are essentially circular journeys which return them to where they began. McTeague returns to the mountains of his youth and stands dumb and brute-like before their primeval enmity; Carrie still rocks and dreams of a happiness she is never to gain; and Fleming is again poised between gratuitous self-assurance and half-concealed doubt.

The form of the naturalistic novel therefore engages us in a somewhat different aesthetic experience than does the form of an archetypal eighteenth or nineteenth-century novel. Whatever the great range of theme and effect of earlier novels, we are more or less instructed and elevated by our experience of their imagined worlds. That deeply gratifying sense of knowing so well the characters of a novel that we are unwilling to part from them at the close of the book is one of the principal effects of a fiction in which the confident moral vision of the writer has encouraged him to depict life with fullness, richness, and direction—with a sense, in short, that both internal and external experience has a kind of describable weight and value. But the form of the naturalistic novel begins to create an effect of uncertainty, of doubt and perplexity, about whether anything can be gained or learned from experience—indeed, of wonder if experience has any meaning aside from the existential value of a collision with phenomena. For what do the massively ironic symbols of McTeague's gold, Carrie's rocking chair, and Fleming's wound tell us but that life is a sliding or drifting rather than a march and that the ultimate direction and possible worth of experience are unfathomable.

If the naturalistic novel is to be properly understood, however, it is necessary to qualify a view which maintains that its major impact is that of the inefficacy of time. For while the naturalistic novel does reflect a vast skepticism about the conventional attributes of experience, it also affirms the significance and worth of the skeptical or seeking temperament, of the character who continues to look for meaning in experience even though there probably is no meaning. This quality appears most clearly in Dreiser's portrayal of Carrie, who, whatever the triviality of her earlier quest or the fatuousness of her final vision, still continues to seek the meaning she calls happiness. It is present in a more tenuous form in the fact that Henry has survived his first battle—that is, his first encounter with life in all its awesome complexity—and is undismayed by the experience. And it exists faintly in the recollection we bring to McTeague's fate of his earlier responsiveness to the promise of Trina's sensuality and to the minor pleasures of middle class domesticity. So the Carrie who rocks, the Fleming who is proud of his red badge, and the McTeague who stands clutching his gold in the empty desert represent both the pathetic and perhaps tragic worth of the seeking, feeling mind and the inability of experience to supply a meaningful answer to the question which is human need. The naturalistic symbol thus accrues to the protagonist a vital ambivalence. It is both a sign of his identity, in that it represents the static reality of his goal or quest in an uncertain, shifting world, and it is a sign of the impossiblity of fulfilling goals or of discovering meaning in a world of this kind.

Since I have been discussing the naturalistic novel in relation to some basic changes in the form of fiction, it would be useful to look forward to the modern novel in order to clarify the significant connection between the fumbling and tentative efforts of the naturalists to reflect through form a new vision of experience and the conscious and sophisticated formalistic experiments by many twentieth-century novelists which have been directed toward achieving a similar end. Obviously, some of the most distinctive qualities of the fiction of Norris, Dreiser, and Crane are in the mainstream of the nineteenth-century novel—the full documentation of Norris and Dreiser, for example, and the arch cleverness of Crane's narrative voice at its worst. Yet by again concentrating on the naturalistic symbol, we can see, I think, how the naturalistic novel stands on the threshold of the modern novel. First, as Richard Ellmann reminds us, one of the basic qualities of Joyce's fiction is his demonstration that "the ordinary is the extraordinary,"[3] that the movement of two men through a commonplace June day in Dublin contains a universe of emotional force and moral implication, though this universe may be expressed by such symbolic acts as those of masturbation and defecation. The gold tooth, rocking chair, and superficial head wound are also commonplace, even tawdry objects and events which symbolize complex and elemental emotions of pride, desire, and fear. Second, the ironic symbolic structure of the naturalistic novel anticipates the absence in much modern serial art of a progressive and developmental notion of time. Because Carrie is still rocking, because McTeague has returned to his original animal state (original both to him and to his species), and because Fleming, despite his wound, is still naively self-deceptive, we realize that time in the shape of experience has been less useful for these characters than it had been for a Dorothea Brooke or a Hester. Soon, indeed, novelists such as Joyce and Virginia Woolf and Faulkner were to discover even more innovative and radical ways to represent through form the insignificance of the forward movement of time in comparison to the timelessness which is the union of a character and his past.

I can perhaps now suggest, after having glanced both backwards and forwards, that the distinctiveness of the form of the naturalistic novel lies in the attempt of that form to persuade us, in the context of a fully depicted concrete world, that only the questioning, seeking, timeless self is real, that the temporal world outside the self is often treacherous and always apparent. The naturalistic novel thus reflects our doubts about conventional notions of character and experience while continuing to affirm through its symbolism both the sanctity of the self and the bedrock emotional reality of our basic physical nature and acts. Put in terms of the history of art, the late nineteenth-century naturalistic novel anticipates both the startling, convention-destroying concreteness and the profound solipsism of much modern art.

At this point we can usefully return to Cady and those other critics who have approached naturalism primarily in relation to its origin and ideas and can note the value of this approach once the stylistic distinctiveness and direction of the naturalistic novel have been established. The influence of Darwinism and French fiction, the notion that man is a brute and life a struggle, the belief that we are but ciphers in either a cosmic storm or a chemical process—this kind of awareness about what the naturalists absorbed and believed can help clarify our understanding of the themes which preoccupied individual naturalists in the muddy pool which is the coming together of a particular temperament and a historical moment. We need not ask which came first or which was predominant— the temperament, the overt beliefs and influences of the age, or the unconscious stumbling of a generation toward a different kind of fictional form. We need only realize that for this particular moment in literary history we have been neglecting the last as a way of controlling and shaping our awareness of the first two. We neglect at our peril the fact that *Moby Dick*, whatever else it may be, is a story of a whale hunt, and we are also in danger, critically speaking, when we neglect the equally simple observation that most late nineteenth-century naturalistic novels are about people who seem to be going nowhere.

4

American Literary Naturalism:
The Example of Dreiser

A MERICAN LITERARY NATURALISM has almost
always been viewed with hostility. During its early
years the movement was associated with Continental licen-
tiousness and impiety and was regarded as a literature foreign to American values and interests. "We must stamp out
this breed of Norrises," a reviewer of *McTeague* cried in
1899.[1] In our own time, though antagonism to naturalism is
expressed more obliquely, it is as deeply rooted. A typical discussion of the movement is frequently along the following
lines.[2] The critic will examine the sources of naturalism in
late nineteenth-century scientism, in Zola, and in post-Civil
War industrial expansion. He will note that to a generation of
American writers coming of age in the 1890s the mechanistic
and materialistic foundations of contemporary science appeared to be confirmed by American social conditions and to
have been successfully applied to the writing of fiction by
Zola. But he will also note that Stephen Crane, Frank Norris,
and Theodore Dreiser were often muddled in their thinking
and inept in their fiction, and he will attribute these failures

to their unfortunate absorption of naturalistic attitudes and beliefs. Our typical critic will then discover a second major flowering of naturalism in the fiction of James T. Farrell, John Steinbeck, and John Dos Passos in the 1930s. He will remark that scientism has been replaced by Marxism and that the thinking of this generation of naturalists is not so much confused as doctrinaire, but his account of their work will still be governed by the assumption that naturalism is a regrettable strain in modern American literary history.

Indeed, the underlying metaphor in most accounts of American fiction is that naturalism is a kind of taint or discoloration, without which the writer would be more of an artist and through which the critic must penetrate if he is to discover the essential nature and worth of the writer. So those writers who most clearly appear to be naturalists, such as Dreiser and Farrell, are almost always praised for qualities which are distinct from their naturalism. We are thus told that Dreiser's greatness is not in his naturalism[3] and that he is most of all an artist when not a philosopher.[4] And so the obvious and powerful thread of naturalism in such major figures as Hemingway, Faulkner, and (closer to our own time) Saul Bellow is almost always dismissed as an irrelevant and distracting characteristic of their work.

This continuing antagonism to naturalism has several root causes. One of the clearest is that many critics find naturalistic belief morally repugnant. But whereas earlier critics stated openly their view that naturalism was invalid because man was as much a creature of divine spirit as animal substance, the more recent critic is apt to express his hostility indirectly by claiming that naturalistic novelists frequently violate the deterministic creed which supposedly informs their work and are therefore inconsistent or incoherent naturalists. On one hand, this concern with philosophical consistency derives from the naturalist writer's interest in ideas and is therefore a justifiable critical interest. On the other, there seems little doubt that many critics delight in seeking out the philosophically inadequate in naturalistic fiction because man is frequently portrayed in this fiction as irredeemably weak and deluded and yet as not responsible for his condition. It is the rare work of fiction of any time in which threads of free will and determinism do not interweave in a complex pattern that can be called incoherent or inconsistent; on strictly logical grounds man either has free will or he does not. Yet it is principally the naturalistic novel which is damned for this quality, which suggests that it is the weighting of this inconsistency toward an amoral determinism—not its mere presence—that is at stake.[5]

Another source of the hostility of modern critics to the naturalistic novel lies in recent American political history. American naturalism of the 1890s was largely apolitical, but in the 1930s the movement was aligned with the left wing in American politics and often specifically with the Communist Party. In the revulsion against the Party which swept the literary community during the 1940s and 1950s, it was inevitable that naturalistic fiction of the 1930s would be found wanting because the naturalists of that decade, it was now seen, had so naively embraced some form of communist belief. The most influential critical discussions of American naturalism during the 1940s and 1950s—Philip Rahv's "Notes on the Decline of American Naturalism," Malcolm Cowley's "A Natural History of American Naturalism," and Lionel Trilling's "Reality in America"[6]—have as an underlying motive a desire to purge American literature and its historiography of an infatuation with an alien and destructive political ideal.

A final reason for the antagonism toward naturalistic fiction is that several generations of academic critics have been attracted by an increasingly refined view of the aesthetic complexity of fiction. They have believed that a novel must above all be organic—that is, the product of a romantic imagination—and they have found principally in the work of Hawthorne, Melville, Faulkner, and to a lesser extent James, that enlargement of metaphor into symbol and that interplay of irony and ambivalence which bring fiction close to the complex indirection of a metaphysical lyric. Stephen Crane is the only naturalistic writer whose fiction satisfies these expectations, and his work is generally held to be uncharacteristic of the non-artistry of a movement more adequately represented by Dreiser.[7]

I do not wish to suggest by this brief survey of the critical biases which have led to the inadequate examination of American naturalism that there are not naturalistic novels which are muddled in conception and inept in execution. But just as we have long known that the mind-set of an early nineteenth–century critic would little prepare him to come to grips with the essential nature and form of a romantic poem, so we are coming to realize that a generation of American critics has approached American literary naturalism with beliefs about man and art which have frequently distorted rather than cast light upon the object before them.

Theodore Dreiser is the author whose work and career most fulfill the received notion of American naturalism; indeed, it is often difficult to determine the demarcation between literary history and critical biography in general discussions of American naturalism, so completely is Dreiser as thinker and writer identified with the movement in America. It would be instructive, therefore, to test the example of Dreiser—to note, initially and briefly, those characteristics of his career and work which lead us to describe him as a naturalist; and then, more fully, to examine some of the naturalistic elements in his fiction. But unlike so much of the criticism of naturalism which I have been describing, I do not wish to undertake this test with the assumption that Dreiser's fiction is confused in theme and form because he is not a consistent naturalist or that his work is best when he is least naturalistic. In short, I do not wish to consider his naturalism as an unfortunate excrescence. Rather, I want to see how his naturalistic predispositions work in his fiction and whether or not they work successfully.

Dreiser was born an outsider. His parents were of Catholic, German-speaking immigrant stock and throughout Dreiser's youth the large family was agonizingly poor. As a young man Dreiser sought the success and position which his parents had lacked and also shed the religious and moral beliefs which, he believed, had appeared to shackle them. While a young reporter in Pittsburgh in the early 1890s, he found his deepest responses to life confirmed by his reading of Herbert Spencer and Balzac. There were, he believed, no discernible supernatural agencies in life, and man was not the favored creature of divine guidance but an insignificant unit in a universe of natural forces. Although these forces, whether biological or social, were the source of racial progress, they often crushed the individual within their mechanistic processes. Like many of his generation, Dreiser found that the observed realities of American society supported this theory of existence. The mills and libraries of Pittsburgh were evidence of progress, but the lives of the immigrant foundry workers—to say nothing of the lives of Dreiser's own errant sisters and brothers—appeared dwarfed and ephemeral compared with the grinding and impersonal power of a vast economic system and a great city. Yet the city itself, as Balzac had amply demonstrated, was exciting and alluring, and not all were crushed who sought to gain its wonders. In *Sister Carrie* Dreiser was to write, "Among the forces which sweep and play throughout the universe, untutored man is but a wisp in the wind."[8] But though Hurstwood is swept away by these forces, and though Carrie's career is that of a storm-tossed ship, Carrie survives and indeed grows in understanding by the close of the novel. So accompanying Dreiser's endorsement of an amoral determinism there exists a disconcerting affirmation of the traditionally elevating in life—of Carrie, for example, as a figure of "emotional greatness," that is, of imaginative power. Forty-five years after *Sister Carrie* Dreiser joined the Communist Party while celebrating in his last two novels the intuitive mysticism at the heart of Quaker and Hindu belief. Here, in brief, at the two poles of his career and work is the infamous intellectual muddle of Dreiser and, by extension, of naturalism itself. And this muddle appears to be matched by a corresponding lack of control and firmness in fictional technique. Dreiser documents his social scene with a pseudo-scientific detachment yet overindulges in personal philosophical disquisitions; he attempts to write a "fine" style but produces journalistic cliché and awkwardness.

So in most important ways Dreiser fulfills the conventional definition of the American naturalist. All the major paradoxes are present: his identification with the "outsider," which was to lead to a contemptuous view of the mainstream of middle class American life, yet his lifelong worship of "success"; his acceptance of a "scientific" mechanistic theory of natural law as a substitute for traditional views of individual insight and moral responsibility, yet his affirmation of many of these traditional views; and his deep response to a major European novelist, including the form of his fiction, yet his seeming neglect of style and form. I cannot hope to discuss these major characteristics of Dreiser as a naturalist as each appears in his eight novels. But I can pursue the vital naturalistic theme of mechanistic determinism in two of his principal novels, *Jennie*

Gerhardt and *An American Tragedy*, and thereby reach toward at least a modest understanding of the example of Dreiser.[9]

Dreiser began *Jennie Gerhardt* in early 1901, soon after the publication of *Sister Carrie*. He wrote most of the novel during the next two years, though he did not complete it until late 1910. Like *Sister Carrie, Jennie Gerhardt* is about a girl from a poor family who has several sexual affairs with men of higher station but who emerges from her adventures not only unsullied but also elevated in character and insight. The novel differs from *Sister Carrie* primarily in Dreiser's characterization of Jennie and of Lester Kane, the principal man in Jennie's life. Kane, at least on the surface, is a more powerful, successful, and contemplative figure than Hurstwood, and Jennie differs from Carrie in that she is a warm and generous giver rather than a taker.

In the course of the novel, Jennie is seduced first by Senator Brander, by whom she has a child, Vesta, and then by Lester Kane. She and Kane are attracted to each other by a powerful natural "affinity" and they live together contentedly for several years. But because Lester is gradually forced to accept that a permanent union with Jennie would adversely affect his business career and the comfortable certainties of his social and family life, they do not marry. Eventually they part, Lester marries Letty Gerald, a woman of his own class, and Jennie suffers the death of both her father and Vesta.

One of the major scenes in *Jennie Gerhardt* is Lester's visit to Jennie after the death of Vesta. Deeply depressed by Vesta's death and by his realization that he erred in leaving Jennie, Lester tells her "it isn't myself that's important in this transaction [that is, life itself] apparently; the individual doesn't count much in the situation. I don't know whether you see what I'm driving at, but all of us are more or less pawns.

We're moved about like chessmen by circumstances over which we have no control."[10] This famous pronouncement, which has supplied several generations of literary historians with a ubiquitous image for the philosophical center of American naturalism, requires careful analysis both in its immediate context and in relation to the novel as a whole if it is to be properly understood.

Whatever the general truth of Lester's words, they represent a personal truth. His pawn image expresses both his sense of ineffectuality in the face of the central dilemma of his life and a covert supernaturalism which has characterized his thought throughout the novel despite his overt freethinking. Earlier he had attributed his difficulties merely to bad luck. But by the time he and Jennie separate, he has elevated and generalized "fate" into a specific force which is at once social, supernatural, and (as far as he is concerned) malevolent:

It was only when the storms set in and the winds of adversity blew and he found himself facing the armed forces of convention that he realized he might be mistaken as to the value of his personality, that his private desires and opinions were as nothing in the face of a public conviction; that he was wrong. The race spirit, or social avatar, the "Zeitgeist" as the Germans term it, manifested itself as something having a system in charge, and the organization of society began to show itself to him as something based on possibly a spiritual, or, at least, supernatural counterpart. (373–74)

Lester's speculative statement that men are but pawns in the control of circumstances is thus in part an explanation and a defense of his own conduct. In particular, it is a disguised apology to Jennie for his failure to marry her when he could have done so. But it is also a powerful means of characterizing Lester. Throughout his life he had lived for the moment and had postponed making decisions about the direction of

his life. But the decisionless flow of time contained an impe-
tus of events which constituted an implicit and irreversible
decision, and when Lester at last awoke to the fact that his life
had been decided for him, he bitterly and angrily blamed
fate.

Because Lester is a perceptive and on the whole an honest
figure, his belief that men are pawns involves more than a rationalization of his own indecisiveness and ineffectuality. His
belief also aptly characterizes social reality as that reality has
been dramatized in the novel. The pressure of circumstances
on Lester in his relationship with Jennie has indeed been intense, from their initial meeting within the convention of a
seduction—a convention which appeared to preclude marriage—to the later opposition of Lester's personal, business,
and social worlds to the continuation of the relationship. In a
passage cut from Chapter XL of the final holograph of the
novel, Dreiser himself, as narrator, echoed Lester's attribu-
tion of superhuman powers to social force. "The conventions
in their way," he wrote, "appear to be as inexorable in their
workings as the laws of gravitation and expansion. There is a
drift to society as a whole which pushes us on in a certain direction, careless of the individual, concerned only with the
general result."[11]

In his final position as one deeply puzzled by the insignificance of the individual, Lester therefore reflects a persistent
strain in Dreiser's thought. Before making his pawn speech
to Jennie, Lester had "looked down into Dearborn Street,
the world of traffic below holding his attention. The great
mass of trucks and vehicles, the counter streams of hurrying
pedestrians, seemed like a puzzle. So shadows march in a
dream" (400). The scene effectively images both Lester's and
Dreiser's belief that life is a helter-skelter of activity without
meaning either for its observers or for the "shadows" who

give it motion. As a man aware of the direction of modern thought, Lester is able to give this view of life an appropriate philosophical framework. In the years that pass after Vesta's death, his response to life, Dreiser tells us, becomes "decidedly critical":

He could not make out what it was all about. In distant ages a queer thing had come to pass. There had started on its way in the form of evolution a minute cellular organism which had apparently reproduced itself by division, had early learned to combine itself with others, to organize itself into bodies, strange forms of fish, animals, and birds, and had finally learned to organize itself into man. Man, on his part, composed as he was of self-organizing cells, was pushing himself forward into comfort and different aspects of existence by means of union and organization with other men. Why? Heaven only knew. . . . Why should he complain, why worry, why speculate?—the world was going steadily forward of its own volition, whether he would or no. Truly it was. (404–05)

It must not be assumed, however, that Lester's pessimistic response to the "puzzle" of man's role in a mechanistic world is Dreiser's principal and only philosophical theme in *Jennie Gerhardt*. For Jennie, though not Lester's equal in formal knowledge or in experience, is his equal in the "bigness" of her responsiveness to the underlying reality of life, and she discovers not only puzzlement and frustration in life but also an ineradicable beauty. Dreiser therefore follows his comments on Lester's critical outlook with an account of Jennie's final evaluation of life. This evaluation, because of its source and its strategic location, has significance equal to Lester's beliefs. Jennie, Dreiser writes,

had never grasped the nature and character of specialized knowledge. History, physics, chemistry, botany, geology, and sociology were not fixed departments in her brain as they were in Lester's and Letty's. Instead there was the feeling that the world moved in some strange, unstable way. Apparently no one knew clearly what it was all about. People were born and died. Some believed that the world had been made six thousand years before; some that it was millions of years old. Was it all blind chance or was there some guiding intelligence—a God? Almost in spite of herself she felt that there must be something—a higher power which produced all the beautiful things—the flowers, the stars, the trees, the grass. Nature was so beautiful! If at times life seemed cruel, yet this beauty still persisted. The thought comforted her; she fed upon it in her hours of secret loneliness. (405)

Jennie and Lester's complementary views of life represent Dreiser's own permanent unresolved conception of the paradox of existence. To both figures the world "was going steadily forward of its own volition," apparently guided by some unknowable power. Individuals counted for little in this process, but individuals of different temperaments might respond to the mechanism of life in different ways. One kind of temperament might be bitter and despairing, another might affirm the beauty which was inseparable from the inexplicable mystery of life. It has frequently been noted that Dreiser himself held both views at different stages of his career—that he stressed a cruelly indifferent mechanistic universe in *Hey Rub-a-Dub-Dub* (1920) and a mechanistic world of beauty in *The Bulwark* (1946). It has not been as fully realized that he held the two positions simultaneously as well as consecutively and that he gave each position equal weight and dramatic expression in *Jennie Gerhardt* without resolving their "discrepancy." For to Dreiser there was no true discrepancy; there was only the reality of distinctive temperaments which might find truth in each position or, as in his own case, of a temperament which might find an element of truth in both. Dreiser's infamous philosophical inconsistency is thus frequently a product of his belief that life is a "puzzle" to which one can respond in different ways, depending on one's makeup and experience.

The naturalistic "philosophy" of deterministic mechanism in Dreiser's novels is therefore usually secondary, within the fictional dynamics of each novel, to the role of the concept as a metaphor of life against which various temperaments can define themselves. Or, to put the matter another way, Lester's belief in one kind of mechanistic philosophy and Jennie's in another are less significant fictionally than the depiction of Jennie as a woman of feeling and of Lester as a man of speculative indecision. But it should also be clear that in attributing a secondary fictional role to the mechanistic center of *Jennie Gerhardt* I am not saying that the philosophy muddles the novel or that the novel is successful for reasons other than the philosophy. I am rather saying that the philosophy and the fiction are one and inseparable. As a late nineteenth-century novelist, Dreiser absorbed and used naturalistic ideas. But he did not do so, at his best, in a way which can be distinguished from his absorption of an understanding of character and of experience in general. It is this unity of understanding and of purpose which gives Dreiser's novels their power. At his most successful, Dreiser embodies in his novels the permanent in life not despite the ideas of his own time but because, like most major artists, he uses the ideas of his own time as living vehicles to express the permanent in man's character and in man's vision of his condition and fate.

Most students of American literature are aware that Dreiser derived the central plot and much of the detail of *An American Tragedy* from the Chester Gillette-Grace Brown murder case of 1906. Less commonly known is that although Dreiser's principal source—the reports of Gillette's trial in the *New York World*—presented him with a wealth of detail about Gillette's life in Cortland (the Lycurgus of the novel) leading up to the murder of Grace Brown, it offered only a few hints about Gillette's experiences before his arrival in that city. Thus, Book One of *An American Tragedy*, which deals with Clyde's early life in Kansas City, is in a sense "invented." Such major events of this portion of the novel as Clyde's sister's pregnancy, his job at the Green-Davidson Hotel, his longing for Hortense, and the automobile accident which concludes the book have no source in Gillette's life.

Because Dreiser in Book One is "inventing" a background for Clyde it is possible to view this section of the novel as the application to fiction of a simplistic deterministic ethic in which the author crudely manufactures hereditary and environmental conditions that will irrevocably propel the protagonist toward his fate. So, in Book One, we are offered Clyde's weak and fuzzy-minded father and coldly moralistic mother. We discover that Clyde is a sensitive youth who longs for the material and sensual pleasures of life but lacks the training, strength, and guile necessary to gain them. Ergo: weakness and desire on the one hand and irresistible attraction yet insurmountable barriers on the other will resolve themselves into an American tragedy.

Dreiser in this opening section of the novel is indeed seeking to introduce the deterministic theme that a young man's nature and early experience can solidify into an inflexible quality of mind which will lead to his destruction. Yet once said this observation is as useless to criticism as the equally true statement that *King Lear* is about the failure and triumph of love. For Dreiser in Book One of *An American Tragedy* is not a simple and simple-minded naturalist applying a philosophical theory to documentary material but rather a subtle fictional craftsman creating out of the imagined concrete details of a life an evocative image of the complex texture of that life.

Clyde's desire for "beauty and pleasure"[12] in Book One is in direct conflict with his parents' religious beliefs and activities, and thus Clyde's dominant impulse from early boyhood is to escape. At fifteen he makes his first major break from his parents' inhospitable mission existence and toward the life he desires when he gets a job as assistant clerk at a drugstore soda fountain. This position, with its accompanying "marvels" of girls, lively talk, and "snappy" dressing, offers a deeply satisfying alternative to the drab religiosity of Clyde's boyhood. He recognizes the appeal of this new world "in a revealing flash": "You bet he would get out of that now. He would work and save his money and be somebody. Decidedly this simple and yet idyllic compound of the commonplace had all the luster and wonder of a spiritual transfiguration, the true mirage of the lost and thirsting and seeking victim of the desert." (I, 26)

Dreiser's summary of Clyde's response to the lively worldliness of the soda fountain introduces a theme, and its imagery and tone, which pervades the entire novel. Clyde's need—his thirst—has the power to transform "spiritually" the tawdry and superficial world of the drugstore into the wondrous and exalted. So frequent and compelling is Dreiser's use of "dream" in connection with Clyde's longing that we sometimes fail to realize that his desires also have a basically religious context in which his "dream" is for a "paradise" of wealth and position ruled by a "goddess" of love. Clyde at this moment of insight at the soda fountain is truly converted. He has rejected the religion of his parents only to find a different kind of heaven to which he pledges his soul with all the fervor and completeness of his parents' belief. Yet like their "cloudy romance" of a heaven above, Clyde's vision of a "paradise" below is a "true mirage." He has thus not really escaped from his parents, and his initiation into life at the soda fountain and later at the Green-Davidson is no true initiation, for he has merely shifted the nebulous and misdirected longings of his family from the unworldly to the worldly. He still has the naïveté, blindness, and absolute faith of his parents' enthusiasm and belief. And because he is, like them, a true believer, he does not learn from experience and he does not change.

Clyde's job as a bellhop at the Green-Davidson is both an extension and an intensification of his conversion experience at the soda fountain. To Clyde, the hotel is "so glorious an institution" (I, 33), a response which at once reflects the religiosity of its sexual attractions and their embodiment in a powerful social form. The Green-Davidson has both an intrinsic and an extrinsic sexuality. So deep and powerful is Clyde's reaction to its beauty and pleasure—to its moral freedom, material splendor, and shower of tips—that he conceives of the hotel as a youth does his first love. The Green-Davidson to Clyde is softness, warmth, and richness; it has a luxuriousness which he associates with sensuality and position—that is, with all that is desirable in life: "The soft brown carpet under his feet; the soft, cream-tinted walls; the snow-white bowl lights set in the ceiling—all seemed to him parts of a perfection and a social superiority which was almost unbelievable" (I, 42). "And there was music always—from somewhere" (I, 33). Clyde thus views the hotel both as "a realization of paradise" and as a miraculous gift from Aladdin's lamp, two images of fulfillment which, in their "spiritualizing" of his desires, appropriately constitute the center of his dream life.

But the hotel has a harsh and cruel sexuality in addition to its soft, warm and "romantic" sensuality. Older women and homosexuals prey on the bellhops, who themselves frequent whores, and the hotel offers many instances of lascivious parties on the one hand and young girls deserted by their seducers on the other. Clyde, because of his repressed sexuality, cannot help responding to this aspect of sex with "fascination" despite his fears and anxieties. The sexual reality of the hotel is thus profoundly ambivalent. Clyde longs above all for the "romance" of sex and for warmth and a sense of union, but the overt sexuality which he in fact encounters is that of hardness, trickery, and deceit—of use and discarding. Both Clyde's unconscious need and his overt mode of fulfillment join in his response to Hortense. "'Your eyes are just like soft, black velvet,'" he tells her. "'They're wonderful.' He was thinking of an alcove in the Green-Davidson hung with black velvet" (I, 112). Clyde unconsciously desires "softness" and later finds it in Roberta, but he is also powerfully drawn by the "hardness" of wealth and sexual power which he is to find in Sondra and which he first encounters at the Green-Davidson. Thus he endows Hortense with an image of warm softness which reflects his muddled awareness of his needs. For though Hortense is properly associated in his mind with the Green-Davidson because of their similar sexual "hardness," she is incorrectly associated with an image of softness and warmth.

Clyde's belief that the Green-Davidson is a "glorious . . . institution" also represents his acceptance of the hotel as a microcosm of social reality. So he quickly learns that to get ahead in the world—that is, to ingratiate himself with his superiors and to earn large tips—he must adopt various roles. So he accepts the hierarchy of power present in the elaborate system of sharing tips which functions in the hotel. So he realizes that he must deceive his parents about his earnings if he is to have free use of the large sums available to him as an eager novice in this institution. And because the world of the Green-Davidson—both within the hotel and as hotel life extends out into Clyde's relations with the other bellhops and with Hortense—also contains Clyde's introduction into sexual desire and sexual warfare, he assumes that the ethics of social advance and monetary gain are also those of love. Thus, when in Lycurgus he aspires to the grandeur of Sondra and her set, his actions are conditioned by an ethic derived from the Green-Davidson—that hypocrisy, dishonesty, role-playing, and sexual deceit and cruelty are the ways in which one gains what one desires and that these can and should be applied to his relationship with Roberta.

The major point to be made about Dreiser's rendering of the Green-Davidson Hotel as an important experience in Clyde's life is that we respond to his account not as an exercise in determinism but as a subtle dramatization of the ways in which a distinctive temperament—eager, sensitive, emotional, yet weak and directionless—interacts with a distinctive social setting which supplies that temperament with both its specific goals and its operative ethic. Again, as in *Jennie Gerhardt*, there is a naturalistic center to this fictional excellence. It is correct to say that Clyde's life is determined by his heredity and environment. But, once more, as in *Jennie Gerhardt*, the naturalism and the fictional strength are inseparable. The naturalism is not an obstacle to the excellence but the motive thrust and center of the bed-rock fictional portrayal of how people interact with their worlds and why they are what they are.

To sum up. One of the major conventions in the study of American naturalism is that naturalistic belief is both objectionable in its own right and incompatible with fictional quality. But the example of Dreiser reveals that the strength often found in a naturalistic novel rests in the writer's commitment to the distinctive form of his naturalistic beliefs and in his ability to transform these beliefs into acceptable character and event. We are moved by the story of Jennie and Lester and by the account of Clyde's career not because they are independent of Dreiser's deepest beliefs but rather because they are successful narratives of man's impotence in the face of circumstances by a writer whose creative imagination was all of a piece. Until we are willing to accept that the power of a naturalistic writer resides in his naturalism, we will not profit from the example of Dreiser.

5

The Problem of Philosophy in the Naturalistic Novel

M Y STARTING POINT is the unalarming but often
ignored premise that there is an important difference between studying a writer's philosophy as a system of
ideas and examining a specific novel by him as a philosophical novel—that is, as a work in which an ideology explicitly
expressed by the author within the novel serves as a means of
explicating and evaluating the novel. This issue in the interpretation of fiction is especially pertinent to the criticism of
the naturalistic novel, since naturalistic fiction—as in much
of the work of Frank Norris and Theodore Dreiser—often
contains quasi-philosophical discourse that is both blatantly
intrusive and puerile in content. To properly criticize this
kind of naturalistic fiction it is necessary, I would suggest, to
recognize that ideas in fiction are not always what they seem
to be.

The first point I would like to make about philosophical
ideas in fiction is that they can serve as metaphors as well as
discursive statements. Ideas of this kind are a special form of

"objective correlative"—special because we usually associate that term with the concrete image. Their principal role in a novel is not to articulate a particular philosophy at a particular moment but rather to contribute to an emotional reality in the work as a whole. We have come to realize that ideas have played such metaphoric roles in other literary forms in earlier literary periods. We are no longer likely to discuss Alexander Pope primarily as a spokesman for specific eighteenth-century philosophical or literary beliefs, though these beliefs are expressed by Pope in his poems. Rather, we now recognize that Pope's beliefs represent metaphoric equivalents of certain perennial states of mind and that it is these equivalents which constitute the permanent poetic thrust of his work.

We have not, however, recognized that ideas in the modern philosophical novel can be interpreted as we have interpreted ideas in earlier and different literary forms. Indeed, the fact that there is a subgenre of modern fiction called "the novel of ideas" implies that ideas in fiction are a special literary phenomenon and that philosophical fiction is thus a special class of fiction. There are several reasons for this failure to recognize the similarity between the role of ideas in fiction and in other literary forms. The ability of the novelist to engage in lengthy philosophical discourse leads us initially to think of his ideas principally as ideas. In addition, the modern novel often expresses ideas which—unlike those of Pope—are either familiar or viable. Thus, when Thomas Mann or D. H. Lawrence voices an idea about politics or about love, his reader is apt to consider the statement as above all an idea about politics or love. He is less apt to realize that the idea might have the same relationship to the theme and form of the novel as a particular action, character, or setting.

These comments on ideas as metaphors are intended to introduce my first example of ideological expression in fiction, a passage from Frank Norris's *Vandover and the Brute*. The passage occurs at the close of chapter 14 of the novel. Vandover, a young middle-class artist, has been living a debauched life in San Francisco since his return from Harvard. At this point in the novel, he has just discovered that he can no longer draw. His sensual excesses have caused him to contract the disease of general paralysis of the insane (or paresis), an early symptom of which is the loss of finer muscular coordination. On the night that Vandover discovers his illness, he looks over the roofs of the sleeping city and hears a flood of sound, as though from an immense beast. Norris then comments in his own voice:

It was Life, the murmur of the great, mysterious force that spun the wheels of Nature and that sent it onward like some enormous engine, resistless, relentless; an engine that sped straight forward, driving before it the infinite herd of humanity, driving it on at breathless speed through all eternity, driving it on no one knew whither, crushing out inexorably all those who lagged behind the herd and who fell from exhaustion, grinding them to dust beneath its myriad iron wheels, riding over them, still driving on the herd that yet remained, driving it recklessly, blindly on and on toward some far-distant goal, some vague unknown end, some mysterious, fearful bourne forever hidden in thick darkness.[1]

The passage is a statement of the idea that life is a struggle for existence. Life and its agent Nature are depicted mechanistically, as an engine which drives humanity forward, crushing the weak in the process. Although this process is ultimately beneficial, since it presses the race "forward," the primary emphasis in the passage is on the terror and awe–inspiring inexorableness of natural force. The meaning of the passage can be extracted from the novel to attribute a "hard" Darwinian philosophy to Norris, or it can be used as a commentary on the theme of the novel—that Vandover, a "laggard" in the herd of humanity because of his self-indulgence, has been caught up in the processes of nature (in this instance a debilitating disease) and will ultimately be destroyed, as indeed he is. In either instance, the passage is viewed principally as "philosophy"—that is, as an indication that Norris subscribes to a particular belief and that this belief is at the heart of *Vandover and the Brute.*

Vandover and the Brute, however, is only indirectly or secondarily a novel about the struggle for existence. It is primarily a novel about the choices open to the artist in late nineteenth-century America. On the one hand, Norris associated art with man's "higher" self and with effort; it represents man's ability to pursue energetically the life of the spirit. On the other hand, he believed that the artist is often the victim of excessive sensibility and sensual self-indulgence. Norris's ideal artist is close to that depicted by Browning—a figure of robust spirituality who fronts life directly. But Norris's conception of the artist was also colored by the nineteenth-century myth of the demonic, self-destructive artist as that myth reaches from Byron and Poe to Oscar Wilde and the aesthetes of the 1890s. Both of these views are present in *Vandover and the Brute,* but the novel is informed principally by Norris's deep-seated belief that though the Browningesque ideal exists as ideal, most artists are incapable of reaching it and therefore succomb to their demonic tendencies.[2]

Norris's method of dramatizing this belief in *Vandover and the Brute* was to cast Vandover's decline in the form of a middle-class parable. After being introduced to the pleasures of the city, Vandover commits the heinous sin of seducing, getting pregnant, and not marrying a middle-class girl. He then loses the positive influences of Home and a Good Woman, and falls under the dominion of Drink, Gambling, and Disreputable Women until—a second heinous sin—he gambles and dissipates away his inheritance and is left ravaged by disease and poverty. *Vandover* is thus above all a parable of the Way to Hell available to the young American artist in a late nineteenth-century American city.

It is now clear, I trust, that Norris used the idea or philosophy of the struggle for existence in *Vandover and the Brute* primarily to make concrete the dangers inherent in the career of a self-indulgent, middle-class artist. The struggle-for-existence idea in *Vandover,* in other words, is principally an image of fear. Norris does indeed subscribe to the idea as idea, but the major function of this idea in the novel is not to state the idea but to dramatize the emotion. Its role is to make compelling an emotion which exists independent of the idea, an emotion which Norris might have expressed by some other means. His choice of this particular idea as a metaphor of fear was therefore primarily a product both of the contemporary pervasiveness and vitality of the idea and of its adaptability to his own ends.

Much of the critical attack on Norris in recent years has been concentrated on his simpleminded and overstated philosophical ideas. But ideas of this kind can contribute to a novel if they have principally a metaphoric function. Once it is recognized that fear permeates Norris's depiction of the artist, it is necessary to evaluate his philosophical passages dealing with the artist at least in part on the basis of the metaphoric impact of these passages rather than entirely on the basis of their intrinsic superficiality or melodramatic imagery. The philosophy of these passages may indeed be both superficial and overstated, but it can nevertheless successfully communicate the reality of fear. In all, the philosophy of the struggle for existence in *Vandover* should be viewed as a modern critic might view the pastoralism of a Renaissance poet. It should be considered primarily as a device by which the artist can transform a quasi-philosophical idea into evocative metaphor. The artist's success in this endeavor, whether he be Renaissance poet or naturalistic novelist, is more dependent upon his emotional resources and literary skill than on the permanent validity of the idea which serves as his controlling metaphor.

The second point that I intend to make about philosophical ideas in fiction is that such ideas are often inadequate guides to the interpretation of the novel in which they appear. Although the novelist seems to be supplying in a philosophical passage an interpretive key to the events he is portraying, he may have a false or superficial discursive grasp of the meaning of these events. Since an author's explicit commentary can run counter to the dramatic action of a novel, the function of the critic may be to apply yet another critical truism current in the criticism of other literary forms—that an artist is often an unsatisfactory commentator on the meaning of his own work. Again, it is more difficult to apply this dictum to the criticism of fiction than to the interpretation of other forms. An authorial comment within the work itself—as in a philosophical passage in a novel—appears to have more validity than an authorial comment in a letter or an essay. The first kind of comment seems weighty because of its immediacy; the second—removed from the work in time and place—can be viewed more objectively. But the history of literature abounds in examples of writers who are both great artists and inadequate critics of their own work, and we should not permit the presence of an author's philosophy in his novel to obscure the possibility of authorial myopia when we interpret that novel.

The philosophical passage from the work of Thedore Dreiser which I will examine occurs in *Sister Carrie* at the opening of chapter 8. At the close of the previous chapter, Carrie has left the Hansons' Chicago flat to move into a room which Drouet has taken for her. In nineteenth-century sentimental terms, she is soon to decide that a comfortable existence as a fallen woman is preferable to the hard life of a poor but honest working girl. Dreiser begins chapter 8 with a lengthy philosophical commentary on Carrie's action:

Among the forces which sweep and play throughout the universe, untutored man is but a wisp in the wind. Our civilization is still in a middle stage, scarcely beast, in that it is no longer wholly guided by instinct; scarcely human, in that it is not yet wholly guided by reason. On the tiger no responsibility rests. We see him aligned by nature with the forces of life—he is born into their keeping and without thought he is protected. We see man far removed from the lairs of the jungles, his innate instincts dulled by too near an approach to free-will, his free-will not sufficiently developed to replace his instincts and afford him perfect guidance. He is becoming too wise to hearken always to instincts and desires; he is still too weak to always prevail against them. As a beast, the forces of life aligned him with them; as a man, he has not yet wholly learned to align himself with the forces. In this intermediate stage he wavers—neither drawn in harmony with nature by his instincts nor yet wisely putting himself into harmony by his own free-will. He is even as a wisp in the wind, moved by every breath of passion, acting now by his will and now by his instincts, erring with one, only to retrieve by the other, falling by one, only to rise by the other—a creature of incalculable variability. We have the consolation of knowing that evolution is ever in action, that the ideal is a light that cannot fail. He will not forever balance thus between good and evil. When this jangle of free-will and instinct shall have been adjusted, when perfect understanding has given the former the power to replace the latter entirely, man will no longer vary. The needle of understanding will yet point steadfast and unwavering to the distant pole of truth.

In Carrie—as in how many of our worldlings do they not?—instinct and reason, desire and understanding, were at war for the mastery. She followed whither her craving led. She was as yet more drawn than she drew.[3]

The philosophy of the passage combines Spencerian evolutionary ideas and popular "ethical culture" thought, a combination much in vogue among liberal, non-denominational clergymen in the 1890s. Man is pictured as a dualistic creature. He still responds instinctively to life because of his animal heritage, yet he is also capable of rational choice. Nature ("the forces of life") is the absolute moral norm: if man were entirely instinctive in his actions, he would be in accord with that norm; if by free will he could choose the way of nature, he would also be acting correctly. Evolution is progressing in the direction of complete rational choice of nature's way. But at present man often finds himself divided and misled because of the conflicting demands of instinct and reason.

The passage, as becomes obvious in the concluding short paragraph, is an apology for Carrie's impending choice of an immoral life with Drouet. Carrie will sense the "wrongness" of the decision, Dreiser implies, because of the glimmerings of reason. But she is dominated by her instinctive needs—by the fact that Drouet represents at this point the full, rich life of Chicago which her imagination has pictured, and that he will supply shelter, warmth, clothing, and food (as well as appreciation and a kind of love) on a level far superior to that offered by the Hansons and on a level commensurate with her sensual nature, with her "craving for pleasure."[4] These instinctive needs associate Carrie with "the tiger [on whom] no responsibility rests"; but they do not disassociate her actions from moral judgment. Man's "reason" permits him to recognize that Drouet represents an inadequate—that is, immoral—fulfillment of Carrie's instinctive needs. Carrie herself, however, finds her instinctive needs too strong, her reason undeveloped and indecisive, and so she "followed whither her craving led. She was as yet more drawn than she drew."

Dreiser's attempt in the passage is to free Carrie from moral responsibility for her action—to suggest that not only Carrie but most men at this intermediate stage of evolutionary development are more led (and misled) than leading. But the passage also judges Carrie's action even though it does not judge Carrie herself. Going to live with Drouet—that is, sexual immorality—is not the "way of nature," Dreiser suggests. Some day, when evolution has progressed further, the "ideal" and the "distant pole of truth" will unwaveringly guide man, and the unmistakable implication is that they will not guide him toward sexual promiscuity.

The passage is readily understandable in the context of the late 1890s. Dreiser had just depicted his heroine as about to undertake a promiscuous life; his philosophical comments permitted him to placate the moral values of his age. Indeed, his comments also placated his own moral sense, for Dreiser in 1899 was in many ways still a conventional moralist when publicly judging the actions of others. A problem arises, however, if one attempts to apply the meaning of the passage to an interpretation of the dramatic action of the novel as a whole—that is, if one concludes that the reader is supposed to sympathize and identify with Carrie's instinctive drive towards "happiness" and "beauty" throughout the novel while simultaneously condemning the means she uses to achieve these goals. Such an interpretation of the novel as a whole is false. The three men in Carrie's life—Drouet, Hurstwood, and Ames—represent an upward movement on Carrie's part. Drouet introduces Carrie to a middle-class world of comfort, show, and finery; Hurstwood to a world of personal and social power; and Ames to that of the intellect. Each relationship serves to refine Carrie's response to life, to raise her above her previous values and desires to a higher stage of development and awareness. Happiness and beauty will never be hers, Dreiser tells us at the end of the novel, but it is clear that she is at least seeking them at a higher level with Ames than was possible with the Hansons. Within the dramatic context of the novel, therefore, Carrie's two illicit relationships are the opposite of what Dreiser has suggested about such relationships in his philosophical passage. They are moral rather than immoral, since they contribute to Carrie's "spiritual" development. In the course of the novel Dreiser has unconsciously changed his moral norm from one which explicitly condemns specific acts of immorality to one which implicitly renders these acts as moral if they contribute to a larger good.

Dreiser's philosophical comments in chapter 8 play a meaningful fictional role at that particular point of the novel. They contribute to the reader's compassion for Carrie ("a wisp in the wind") while disarming his possible moral judgment of her. The comments, in other words, are part of Dreiser's characterization of Carrie. But if we accept these comments as relevant to the themes of the novel as a whole, we will be interpreting and evaluating *Sister Carrie* on a level appropriate to the articulated conventional moral philosophy of Dreiser's day rather than on the level of Dreiser's inarticulate unconventional sense of the meaning of experience, a sense expressed by the dramatic action of the novel. And it is no doubt Dreiser's responses to life rather than his explicit comments on life which are the source of the "power" that many readers acknowledge in his fiction.

I have been attempting to suggest by means of two philosophical passages in American naturalistic novels that criticism of fiction must explicate such passages as complex fictional constructs rather than respond to them solely as ideas. The literal meaning of such passages may represent only a portion of their meaning (as in *Vandover*) or it may be an inadequate meaning (as in *Sister Carrie*). The presence in fiction of ideas of this kind is not, I believe, an immediate sign of aesthetic weakness. Rather, their presence suggests the rhetorical similarities between fiction and other literary forms in which ideas have always been more or less than ideas. All writers are "makers," and an idea in a novel is as much a "made" object as a character or an event. Our difficulty as critics of naturalistic novels which are also philosophical novels stems in part from our professional intellectuality, since we tend to assume that writers, as intellectuals, do not make ideas but think them. Our task as critics of philosophical fiction, however, requires that we not only understand an idea in a novel but, in a sense, that we refuse to understand it.

6

The Evolutionary Foundation of W. D. Howells's *Criticism and Fiction*

WILLIAM DEAN HOWELLS'S *Criticism and Fiction* has never fared well as literary criticism, though its historical importance has seldom been questioned. In its own time it was a major contribution to the realism-romanticism controversy of the eighties and nineties. As in much literary dispute, examination of the work was usually neglected for criticism based upon a defense of vested literary interests or an a priori antagonism to the new and seemingly radical.[1] Today, the depreciation of *Criticism and Fiction* continues, though of course along different lines. Critics have found the source of its defects in the facts of its composition and publication. The volume was made up of brief, loosely connected critical essays which had originally appeared in other contexts in Howells's "Editor's Study" department in *Harper's Monthly*. Everett Carter, for example considers it a "hastily contrived product of the scissors and the pastepot" lacking clarity and unity.[2] He also contends that Howells's literary principles changed sufficiently from January, 1886 (the date of the first "Editor's Study") to May, 1891 (when *Criticism and Fiction* was published) to invalidate not only the famous "smiling aspects of life" passage but the entire work as well. He points out that during 1886 and 1887 Howells underwent the "agony" of the Haymarket affair and its resultant change in his social and literary views. *Criticism and Fiction,* which contains material written both before and after this crisis, is therefore not an adequate expression of Howells's mature critical realism. He concludes that one has "to look elsewhere for the best expression of his critical opinions."[3]

There is no doubt that *Criticism and Fiction* adversely reflects its original periodical publication. There are obvious transitional gaps and contrivances; the work lacks outward direction and focus; and there is much repetition. But this is not to say that the collection is deficient in a coherent, pervasive, and unified system of ideas which serves as an intellectual base for Howells's critical attitudes. It is a belief in the evolution of literature which underlies the seemingly disparate critical comments of *Criticism and Fiction.* I will first examine the general nature of the use of evolutionary ideas in literary criticism during the 1880s and Howells's own awareness and acceptance of this use.[4] I will then examine the foundation of evolutionary ideas in *Criticism and Fiction.* It should be clear, however, that my analysis of *Criticism and Fiction* is not a defense of its two paramount weaknesses—an undisciplined structure and an over-reliance, for polemic purposes, upon the contemporary belief that evolutionary theories could be applied to an interpretation of literature. Rather, my purpose is to point out the depth of Howells's dependence upon this belief and to indicate that his attitudes toward criticism and fiction are coherent in their common reference to a conception of the evolution of literature.

Perhaps one of the clearest and also most doctrinaire examples of evolutionary literary criticism is an unpublished work by Hamlin Garland, written during 1886–87, entitled "The Evolution of American Thought."[5] At one point in this history of American literature, Garland wrote: "Nothing is stable, nothing absolute, all changes, all is relative. Poetry, painting, the drama, these too are always being modified or left behind by the changes in society from which they spring."[6] This statement contains two of the main tenets of evolutionary criticism—that literature is a product of the society in which it is found; and that literature, like society, is therefore continually in flux. To this basic environmental relativism can be added the idea that change in both society and literature is slowly but inevitably progressive. "The golden age is here and now," Garland summed up, "and the future is a radiant promise of ineffable glory."[7] The primary sources of these ideas, for Garland and for other evolutionary critics of the period, are not far to seek. From Taine came the principle that literature is conditioned by the forces of race, environment, and epoch. From evolutionary science, which itself reinforced an environmental determinism, came the idea that life is continually in flux. And from such popularizers of evolution as Herbert Spencer and John Fiske came the belief that the principle of change was applicable to social, intellectual, and moral—as well as material—life and was characterized by the ultimate achievement of "the greatest perfection and the most complete happiness."[8]

Garland had been influenced directly by Taine and Spencer and also, to a lesser extent, by the criticism of Hutcheson Macaulay Posnett and Thomas Sergeant Perry, two evolutionary critics whose work was also known by Howells. In the Preface to his *Comparative Literature* (1886), Posnett stated that his purpose was "to explain literary development by scienti-

fic principles."[9] The use of these principles involved group-
ing the study of literature

round certain central facts of comparatively permanent influence.
Such facts are the climate, soil, animal and plant life of different
countries; such also is the principle of evolution from communal to
individual life. . . . The former may be called the statical influences
to which literature has been everywhere exposed; the latter may be
called the dynamical principle of literature's progress and decay.[10]

These two "facts"—obviously derived from Taine and Spencer—led Posnett to his central critical belief, that there are no
absolutes in literary form or content. For, he argued, given
the fact that literature depends on physical and social conditions and that these conditions vary in time and place, how
can one maintain that there are absolute standards? Social
life had evolved progressively from the homogeneity of the
clan to the heterogeneity of a modern democracy. And since
literature, if it is to be vital, must reflect this progress, it is
retrogressive to ask the modern writer to conform to standards which were derived by older civilizations. In the body
of his work Posnett examined the progress of world literature
from barbaric times to his own day and concluded with a
celebration of Whitman's "democratic individualism."

Both Garland and Posnett were disciples of Herbert Spencer and attempted to apply Spencerian evolutionary formulas to an interpretation of the "dynamic" in literature. But
T. S. Perry, although he too was influenced by Spencer, revealed that it was not necessary to use a particular evolutionary system, that an awareness of literature's change and
growth could constitute an evolutionary method. His *English
Literature in the Eighteenth Century* (1883), for example, was an
attempt to illustrate "the more evident laws that govern literature."[11] He was at particular pains, in his Preface, to re-

fute Mrs. Oliphant's *Literary History of England in the End of the Eighteenth and Beginning of the Nineteenth Century* (1882). Mrs. Oliphant had accepted the idea of progress in most phases of life but had denied its applicability to literature and art because there had been no advance upon Shakespeare or Fra Angelico. Perry, like most evolutionary critics, conceded that the source and nature of genius were inexplicable. But he argued that genius is nevertheless conditioned by life and that the general drift of life was progressive. The writer

can see only what exists or may exist, and is limited by experience whether this be treated literally or be modified by the imagination. No writer can escape this limitation any more than he can imagine a sixth sense. If these statements are accurate, and a general, although not uniform, progress is acknowledged to exist in society, literature may also be said to be under the sway of law, or, rather, to move in accordance with law.[12]

Like Garland and Posnett, Perry accepted the premises and conclusion of the evolutionary critical syllogism: that literature is conditioned by society; that society progresses; and therefore that literature progresses in the "general widening of human interest and sympathies" which it mirrors, though a genius may be lacking to crystallize this progress into great expression.[13]

But Perry's conception of the "laws that govern literature" contained in addition an idea which was to play an important role in Howells's treatment of literary progress. Perry believed that the progress of society was reflected in literature. But he also accepted John Addington Symonds's belief that literary genres occupied the position of species within the broad pattern of progress and that each genre passed through a life cycle of birth, maturity, and decay.[14] The advantage of this dual conception was that it allowed Perry to postulate the perpetual progress of society and literature, yet also supplied him with an explanation (one of several) for fluctuation in the history of literature. Shakespeare was a genius extant at the apex of his genre's cycle. There might have been comparable geniuses at earlier or later periods in the history of Elizabethan drama, but they were unfortunately limited by the immaturity or decay of the genre. As Perry explained in discussing the Greek drama, Sophocles reached a higher level of achievement than Aeschylus, but the difference between them was "not so much a personal one as it was the necessary result of their relative positions in the history of the Greek drama."[15]

This duality in the conception of the evolution of literature also had the advantage of permitting Perry to establish permanent critical values despite the relativism caused by literature's dependence upon a society continually in flux. Indeed, the relationship between literature and society was the source of these values, for a close relationship was necessary if literature was to represent the progress of society. The progress in any literary genre was therefore not only a growth in technique and form, but also a more truthful representation of the life of its time. Decay occurred when this latter function was neglected or when another genre more able to perform the task arose.

Several studies have documented Howells's knowledge of science and his acceptance of evolutionary ideas, and there is no need for more than a summary here.[16] During his years as an editor and then editor-in-chief of the *Atlantic Monthly* (1866–81), Howells read, reviewed, or editorially supervised many works and articles on Taine and evolution. During these years he also became closely acquainted with John Fiske and Perry, both of whom were Cambridge neighbors and contributors to the *Atlantic*.[17] By the time he began writing the "Editor's Study," Howells fully supported an evolutionary interpretation of literature. In a review of Posnett's *Comparative Literature* in the July, 1886, "Editor's Study," he applauded both Posnett and Perry for their "application of scientific theories to literature" and for their "conscious perception of principles which others have been feeling more or less blindly, and which are really animating and shaping the whole future of criticism." Both critics, he pointed out, hold that "literature is from life, and that it is under the law as every part of life is, and is not a series of preposterous miracles."[18] And in reviews later that year and in 1891 he continued to praise Perry's "scientific methods" which indicate "a new voice, a new temper" in literary criticism.[19]

Criticism and Fiction has little external pattern, but what organization it has suggests its controlling current of ideas. The work consists of an unnumbered introduction and twenty-eight numbered essays. The twenty-eight essays can be divided into two parts: the first thirteen deal primarily with criticism, the last fifteen with fiction. The introductory unnumbered essay is taken up almost entirely with a passage from J. A. Symonds's *Renaissance in Italy,* which Howells quoted as relevant to the problem of establishing enduring critical principles in literature as well as in art. Symonds anticipated that criticism in the future would avoid " 'sentimental or academical seekings after the ideal' " and " 'momentary theories founded upon idiosyncratic or temporary partialities.' " Once this has been accomplished, the role of the critic will be that of " 'a healthy person who has made himself acquainted with the laws of evolution in art and in society, and is able to test the excellence of work in any stage from immaturity to decadence by discerning what there is of truth, sincerity, and natural vigor in it.' "[20] In short, the equipment of the critic will be a rejection of the older critical standards of the ideal and the personal, an acceptance of the principle of evolution in society and literature, and a realization that truth, sincerity, and vigor are the most estimable qualities of literature. Howells's strategic placing of this excerpt encourages the belief that these were to be the methods of his own examination of modern criticism and fiction.

A fundamental postulate of an evolutionary critical system is that literature is a product of the physical, social, and intellectual environment in which it is found and can best be understood and interpreted in terms of its environment. Howells accepted this belief, giving it a nationalistic or racial emphasis, as Taine had done. He explained that the "dispassionate, scientific student" of literature realizes that "it is a plant which springs from the nature of a people, and draws its forces from their life, that its root is in their character, and that it takes form from their will and taste" (55).

Howells also accepted the other major postulates of an evolutionary system—that both society and literature are characterized by change for the better. Society was not only advancing materially, but was achieving a greater humanitarianism and a submersion of the primitive and bestial. Literature also was both mutable and progressive. Fiction, for example, was progressing in two ways, one internally, the other a reflection of progress in society. Internally, in form and technique, it had gradually evolved from crudity and obviousness to subtlety, complexity, and sureness of touch. In subject matter it had increasingly devoted itself to a truthful and sincere account of the affairs of mankind. Society's growing humanitarianism was mirrored in the novel's concern for the truth in human relations in every sphere of life.

Realism was the fictional method which embodied both the technical and the humanitarian progress of fiction. Howells confessed that he liked "better to go forward than to go backward, and it is saying very little to say that I value more such a novel as Mr. James's Tragic Muse than all the romantic attempts since Hawthorne" (118). He believed that the movement from classicism to romanticism to realism was a kind of positivistic progress toward a literature which would attempt to describe life truthfully:

Romanticism then sought [in its struggle against classicism], as realism seeks now, to widen the bounds of sympathy, to level every barrier against aesthetic freedom, to escape from the paralysis of tradition. It exhausted itself in this impulse; and it remained for realism to assert that fidelity to experience and probability of motive are essential conditions of a great imaginative literature. It is not a new theory, but it has never before universally characterized literary endeavor. (15)

Howells's conception of the novel as a developing genre is illustrated by his evaluation of the great novelists of the preceding age. Balzac, Scott, and Dickens were literary geniuses who were nevertheless restricted by the primitive state of the novel during their age. The novel was a slowly progressing species with a particular norm of achievement at a particular moment in time; even the great man could not vary too much from the norm. The barbarian who discovered fire was a genius and was greater than those around him, but he was still a barbarian. "In the beginning of any art even the most gifted worker must be crude in his methods" (21). Writers in the "stone age" (119) of fiction, however, such as Scott and Balzac, were not to be condemned for their flaws in technique and content. Balzac "stood at the beginning of the great things that have followed since in fiction . . . [but] one perceives that Balzac lived too soon to profit by Balzac" (18–19). His technique was "not so bad in him as it would be in a novelist of our day. It is simply primitive and inevitable, and he is not to be judged by it" (20). Even Goethe in his fiction could not rise above the low development of the novel during his age: "What is useful in any review of Goethe's methods is the recognition of the fact . . . that the greatest master cannot produce a masterpiece in a new kind. The novel was too recently invented in Goethe's day not to be, even in his hands, full of the faults of apprentice work" (24).

There remains the primary question of Howells's application of his conception of the evolution of fiction to the contemporary roles of criticism and fiction. Howells assigned criticism a scientific role; its function was not to direct or control the progress of fiction, but rather to describe and analyze fiction on the basis of a realization of the law of progress as it operated in society and literature. Fiction, on the other hand, was creatively to embody a truthful description of contemporary life.

Howells's limitation of the function of criticism denied to it, above all, the right of judgment. The critic had not realized that "it is really his business to classify and analyze the fruits of the human mind very much as the naturalist classifies the objects of his study, rather than to praise or blame them" (30). Most contemporary criticism was marred by judgment based upon personal taste or party and literary prejudice. Too much criticism, moreover, was merely a display of wit and brilliance, in the English fashion.

Howells restricted the role of criticism because it had retarded, by judgments based upon false standards, the natural progress of fiction. In the modern period it was beginning to be seen "that no author is an authority except in those moments when he held his ear close to Nature's lips and caught her very accent" (14). But despite this realization, "criticism does not inquire whether a work is true to life, but tacitly or explicity compares it with models, and tests it by them" (47). Too many readers, misled by criticism and unaware that literature progressed, desired the "ideal grasshopper, the heroic grasshopper, the impassioned grasshopper" (12) which they recalled from the authors of their youth. They judged modern fiction therefore "by a standard taken from these authors, and never dreamed of judging it by nature" (12–13).

Modern criticism was to a large measure responsible for this "petrifaction of taste" which represented a more primitive level of both art and life. Criticism wished literary art to "travel in a vicious circle" rather than a straight line, and to "arrive only at the point of departure" (47). In other words, criticism as a genre was backward; it had not developed sufficiently to realize its place and function. It was distinctly atavistic, for example, in its continuance of anonymous criticism, a "savage condition" which "still persists" despite the advance of manners and courtesy in society (50). But most of all, criticism had not realized that principles and laws function in literature as well as in every phase of life.

Fortunately, the main tendency in world fiction had been progressive, despite the hindrance of much criticism. If criticism still failed to recognize the intrinsic relationship between life and literature, this was not true of most modern fiction. Fiction of the past, however, had been "largely injurious . . . through its falsehood, its folly, its wantonness, and its aimlessness" (93–94). It was therefore a sign of progress that the modern novel was required to answer the question, "Is it true?—true to the motives, the impulses, the principles that shape the life of actual men and women?" (99). Truth was now the "highest mission" of fiction, and though modern fiction was not always equal to the task, "fiction is now a finer art than it has ever been hitherto, and more nearly meets the requirements of the infallible standard" (185–86). This did not mean that fiction was the ultimate form, that it alone could meet the standards of truth and sincerity. On the contrary, it was conceivable that "when the great mass of readers, now sunk in the foolish joys of mere fable, shall be lifted to an interest in the meaning of things through the faithful portrayal of life in fiction, then fiction the most faithful may be superseded by a still more faithful form of contemporaneous history" (186–87). In short, progress was along the line of an increasingly truthful portrayal of life, not only within a genre, but from genre to genre as well.

But if the novel was progressing, why was there so much that was false and romantic in modern fiction? And why, particularly, had English fiction decayed since Jane Austen, who had been "the first and the last" English novelist to treat material with complete truthfulness and was "alone worthy to be matched with the great Scandinavian and Slavic and Latin artists" (73)? As far as the English novel was concerned, this arresting of progress was "not a question of intellect, or not wholly that. The English have mind enough; but they have not taste enough; or, rather, their taste has been perverted by their false criticism, which is based upon personal preference, and not upon principle" (73–74). Of course, the "taint" of romanticism had adversely affected the English novel after Austen and was partially responsible for its decline—"but it really seems as if it were their criticism that was to blame for the rest: not, indeed, for the performance of this writer or that, . . . but for the esteem in which this writer or that is held through the perpetuation of false ideals" (75). The English novel had suffered from the failure of English criticism to realize the principles which govern criticism and fiction and was an outstanding example of the ability of false criticism to hinder the progress of fiction.

With the exception of England, world fiction was advancing in meeting the tests of truth and sincerity. But despite this general advance, Howells noted that certain older, "untruthful" forms of fiction continued to remain popular. He explained that these older types were primitive forms of entertainment which appealed to those who in "every civilized community live in a state of more or less evident savagery" (109). Moreover, even "the most refined, the most enlightened person has his moods, his moments of barbarism. . . . At these times the lettered and the unlettered are alike primitive" (109). The romanticist still appealed because "the world often likes to forget itself, and he brings on his heroes, his goblins, his feats . . . and the poor, foolish, childish old world renews the excitements of its nonage" (107). Though Howells himself acknowledged some pleasure in poetical and historical romances, he admonished that the reader was not to confuse these survivals with the true function of modern fiction; otherwise "we shall be in danger of becoming permanently part of the 'unthinking multitude,' and of remaining puerile, primitive, savage" (111).

One of Howells's principal concerns in *Criticism and Fiction* was to examine the state of contemporary American fiction. He found that on the whole it was playing its role in the progress of world fiction and was representing American life with increasing truthfulness, sincerity, and vigor. American novels, unlike English, had "a disposition to regard our life without the literary glasses so long thought desirable, and to see character, not as it is in other fiction, but as it abounds outside of all fiction" (124).

American fiction, since it viewed American life truthfully, reflected the actual conditions of American life. Howells pointed out that most attacks on American fiction were invalid because the supposed weaknesses were the product of

American conditions. American fiction, for example, lacked the tragic depth of a Dostoevsky because our life consisted primarily of "well-to-do actualities" (129). The idea of the average, the norm, was important here as elsewhere in Howells's conception of the role of American fiction. The writer concerned himself, in his attempt to arrive at the closest possible approximation of the truth, with the most probable, the most characteristic, rather than the anomaly, which might be true to one but not to the average.

Howells's belief that literature more closely approaches truth as it devotes itself to the norm of behavior appears most clearly in his analysis of the treatment of sex in American fiction. He acknowledged that the American novel dealt less openly with sex than either eighteenth-century English or contemporary French fiction. But he considered this absence an advance on two levels. On the one hand, the American novel was again reflecting the progress of society, for the "manners of the novel have been improving with those of its readers" (154). But also, American fiction, by subordinating sex, more accurately represented the true position of sex in life. Contemporary novelists had not denied the role of sex and passion, but had rather "relegated them in their pictures of life to the space and place they occupy in life itself, as we know it in England and America. They have kept a correct proportion" (156).

Another charge against American fiction which Howells refuted was that it was too narrow. Here again he pointed out that the supposed defect was actually a virtue, since it indicated a truthful representation of a condition of American life. American novels were still thorough, but their "breadth is vertical instead of lateral, that is all; and this depth is more desirable than horizontal expansion in a civilization like ours, where the differences are not of classes, but of types, and not of types either so much as of characters. A new method was necessary in dealing with the new conditions" (142). No writer could hope to capture all of American life—"our social and political decentralization forbids this" (144)—and specialization had become necessary.

Lastly, Howells traced the relationship between a democracy and the literature which reflected it. American life had been derided for lacking distinction. But Howells saw such a deficiency as a source of inspiration, not discouragement, for the American writer. American life affirmed "the essential equality of men in their rights and duties" (139). This democratic condition invited the artist "to the study and the appreciation of the common, and to the portrayal in every art of those finer and higher aspects which unite rather than sever humanity, if he would thrive in our new order of things" (139). In his truthful study of the common, the American writer was not to gloss over the inadequacies of American life, its poor and suffering. A truthful fiction describing these weaknesses aided in their amelioration, since it forced men to respond to the spirit of brotherhood implicit in a democracy: "Men are more like than unlike one another; let us make them know one another better, that they may be all humbled and strengthened with a sense of their fraternity" (188). A democratic fiction which would reflect both the fraternity and the lapses from fraternity in American life would be a high-water mark in the progress of fiction.

Criticism and Fiction is no more than a fraction of Howells's total critical writings, and it is perhaps unrepresentative in its polemicism and over-statement, which were products of the atmosphere of controversy in which the original essays were written. Yet the work, despite the additional facts that it is hastily contrived and that it spans a period of vital change in

Howells's social views, is nevertheless an adequate representation of his critical position. Howells believed throughout
his later career as well as in 1886 that American fiction progressed as it came closer to a truthful portrayal of American
life, and that it was the role of criticism to aid, rather than
hinder, this progress. It was Howells's perception of American life—that the smiling aspects were not as characteristic as
he had supposed—which changed, not his conception of the
functions of criticism and fiction.

But *Criticism and Fiction* also illustrates some of the dangers
of the application of a doctrinaire theory—"scientific" or
otherwise—to literary criticism. Howells found in evolution
a means of defending Howellsian realism and attacking his
bêtes noires of English criticism and romantic fiction. Perhaps
such an adaptation is the fate of most sociological or biological theories which are applied to the study of literature in a
controversial context. But evolution—which encouraged the
critic to select contemporary modes and forms and then to interpret literature as a "progress" toward these goals—was
apparently particularly susceptible to this temptation.

7

Evolutionary Ideas in
Late Nineteenth-Century English
and American Literary Criticism

A S WE ENTER fully into the second century of *The Origin of Species* we recognize that the theory of evolution is one of the dominant ideas of recent history and that we have just begun to explore its impact on the world of ideas beyond its manifestation in controversies between science and religion. I would like to offer a sketch of the influence of evolutionary ideas on one portion of that world, that of late nineteenth-century literary criticism in English. I will first outline briefly the various stages of this influence and then discuss the particular ways in which evolutionary ideas contributed to the modification of the study and evaluation of literature in America and England during the last three decades of the century.

It is possible to distinguish three roughly chronological periods in the influence of evolutionary ideas. First, during the 1870s and 1880s certain critics whose thought and values were essentially pre-Darwinian drew upon evolutionary ideas to support preconceived critical and ethical positions. Such writers as Sidney Lanier and E. C. Stedman, for example, paid little heed to the materialistic and deterministic implications of evolutionary science. Rather, they responded to the individualism and optimism of Spencerian evolution and adapted selected portions of evolutionary thought to confirm romantic conceptions of the purpose and value of literature. During the 1880s and 1890s, on the other hand, a number of critics drew more deeply upon evolutionary ideas. Thomas Sergeant Perry, Hamlin Garland, William Morton Payne, John Addington Symonds, and H. M. Posnett relied upon the historical relativism and environmental determinism implicit in the ideas of evolution, and also upon Herbert Spencer's master evolutionary formula, in their attempts to construct fully elaborated evolutionary systems. The last period in the influence of evolutionary ideas began in the 1880s and still continues. Academic critics such as Brander Matthews, H. H. Boyesen, and Edward Dowden, as well as such professional literary men as William Dean Howells and George Pellew, did not go to the extreme of building evolutionary critical systems. Rather, they absorbed into their critical practices and beliefs certain by-products of the evolutionary conception of the nature of literature and the function of the critic. The weary graduate student who today has to read Boileau along with Dryden, who complains of lengthy reading lists consisting of minor works by minor figures, who has to know Trevelyan's *Social History* as well as Baugh's *Literary History*, little realizes that he is at least in part engaged in "the scientific study of literature" as many evolutionary critics of the late nineteenth century conceived of that study.

Evolutionary ideas influenced the study and evaluation of literature in three ways during the late nineteenth century. First, the widely held conviction that the principles of evolution evident in man's biological past could also be found in his intellectual and social past encouraged a belief that litera-

ture grew and changed according to natural law—that literature, like life, was dynamic rather than static, and that its
condition at any one moment of time could be understood
only by an examination of its development from its previous
condition. Secondly, evolutionary ideas supported an emphasis on the milieu as the determining factor in literary production rather than the individual writer. It was the literary
and social environment which conditioned the writer's
ideals, material, and methods and which therefore ultimately
determined the pattern of literary history. Lastly, evolutionary studies fostered a conception of the critic or historian as
an analogue to the scientist—as an analytical observer and
codifier of literary specimens rather than a belletristic enter-
tainer or an arbitrary determiner of value.

Let me examine each of these major patterns of influence
in greater detail. The concept of change is fundamental to
evolutionary thought, and Darwin's belief that biological
change is the product of variation and natural selection was
immediately available as a possible means of examining
change in other phases of man's experience. The application
to literary study of the environmental determinism implicit
in the theory of natural selection was also encouraged, of
course, by Taine's belief that literature is the product of a nation's physical and social conditions. But the basic pattern of
evolutionary change which was joined to Taine's environmental determinism to produce an evolutionary critical system was seldom Darwinian. Rather, most critics accepted
and absorbed Herbert Spencer's doctrine that evolution is, in
all phases of life, a progress from the simplicity of incoherent
homogeneity to the complexity of coherent heterogeneity.
There were several reasons why the Spencerian formula appealed to literary men. It was universally applicable, explicit-

ly optimistic, and easily grasped; it was capable of wide variation depending on the predilections of the individual writer;
and, perhaps most of all as far as American criticism was concerned, it permitted the critic to view the history of literature
as a progress toward a democratic individualism in expression and subject matter.[1]

The combination of Taine and Spencer is therefore the basic pattern in most evolutionary critical systems of the 1880s
and 1890s. A typical example is H. M. Posnett's juxtaposition of the static and the dynamic. Posnett argued that the
critic must organize his studies

> round certain central facts of comparatively permanent influence.
> Such facts are the climate, soil, animal and plant life of different
> countries; such also is the principle of evolution from communal
> [that is, homogeneous] to individual [that is, heterogeneous]
> life. . . . The former may be called the statical influences to which
> literature has been everywhere exposed; the latter may be called the
> dynamical principle of literature's progress and decay.[2]

What Posnett called the dynamic, T. S. Perry named growth
and J. A. Symonds process. "The fundamental conception
which underlies the Evolutionary method of thought," Symonds explained, "is that all things in the universe exist in
process. No other system has so vigorously enforced the truth
that it is impossible to isolate phenomena from their anteced-
ents and their consequents."[3] Like Posnett, Symonds viewed
change in Spencerian terms. "Evolution," he stated, "may
be defined as the passage of all things, inorganic and organic,
by the action of inevitable law, from simplicity to complexity,
from an undifferentiated to differentiated condition."[4] The
belief that literature was largely a product of social conditions, and that these conditions changed according to the
Spencerian formula, is exemplified by Hamlin Garland's un-

published "The Evolution of American Thought." In this work, written during 1886–87, Garland explained that the progress of American literature was dependent upon the growth of heterogeneity in American social and intellectual life.[5] The application of the Spencerian formula is also illustrated by Posnett's organization (in his *Comparative Literature*) of the history of European literature around the progress from the clan to the city-state to the nation to the individual, and by T. S. Perry's conception of the history of the drama. Perry wrote:

The change from a drama that represented only kings and heroes of princely birth to one that concerned itself with human beings, was as inevitable a thing as is the change in government from despotism to democracy, with the growth of the importance of the individual. There is a certain monotony in civilization which may be exemplified in a thousand ways. The large gas pipes, for instance, that are laid in every street, and then have the smaller branches running into every house, which again feed the ramifying tubes that supply the single lights, may remind one of the advance from the general to the particular which characterizes every form of human thought.[6]

But whatever the degree of Spencerianism in particular critics, the primary characteristics of evolutionary criticism were adequately summarized by William Morton Payne when he wrote, "We are coming to understand more and more clearly that . . . the history of literature is the history of a process, and the study of a work of literature is the study of a product. To this, in the last analysis, the evolutionary conception of literature reduces."[7] Hamlin Garland was even more explicit when he stated that "Nothing is stable, nothing absolute, all changes, all is relative. Poetry, painting, the drama, these too are always being modified or left behind by the changes in society from which they spring."[8]

The dynamic quality of literature was not only the result of literature's intrinsic relationship with a society continually in flux. Literature also contained within itself a constantly changing element, one comparable to a species in biological life. Like a species, a literary genre pursued a life cycle from birth to maturity to death and decay. Explanations of the cause of this cycle differed somewhat from critic to critic. William Morton Payne believed that there was a struggle for existence among genres.[9] Symonds and Perry held that the works within a genre inevitably reached a high point, after which they substituted literary imitation for a reflection of life, a failure to adapt to environment which ultimately caused the decline of the genre.[10] The important similarity among all critics employing a genre approach to the evolution of literature was their belief in the subservience of the individual writer to the stage of development of his genre. Writers in the "stone age" of fiction, Howells observed, such as Scott and Balzac, were not to be blamed for their flaws in technique and content.[11] Even Goethe in his fiction could not rise above the low development of the novel during his age. "What is useful in any review of Goethe's methods," Howells wrote, "is the recognition of the fact . . . that the greatest master cannot produce a masterpiece in a new kind. The novel was too recently invented in Goethe's day not to be, even in his hands, full of the faults of apprentice work."[12] T. S. Perry, on the other hand, pointed out that praise was usually unjustified for a later writer in a genre on the basis of his superiority to an earlier. Sophocles reached a greater height than Aeschylus, Perry noted, but he then went on to explain that the difference between them "was not so much a personal one as it was the necessary result of their relative positions in the history of the Greek drama."[13]

The effect of the application to literary study of both the Spencerian conception of progress and the conception of the genre as analogous to a species was to diminish the importance of the author in literary creation. In this tendency evolutionary critics locked horns with the romantic celebration of genius. Many evolutionary critics openly attacked the idea that the genius was above or outside law. They pointed out that the reliance upon an inexplicable outburst of genius as an explanation of literary production was comparable to the reliance placed upon special creation in the explanation of biological existence. T. S. Perry complained that although the idea that it is possible to evoke "something out of nothing by direct exercise of creative power . . . has vanished from science, it still survives in those departments of human activity which have not yet come fully under scientific treatment, and poets and painters enjoy in the popular estimation a privilege which has been denied to nature."[14] The cult of genius was a "mischievous superstition," as Howells put it,[15] which hindered the realization that all writers, whatever their degree of ability, were dependent upon their time and place for inspiration and material.

Of course, most evolutionary critics recognized the existence of literary greatness, a phenomenon which they explained variously as either the result of one extreme in the spectrum of literary ability, or as the literary parallel of "spontaneous variations"—that is, biological sports.[16] Hamlin Garland expressed a typical conception of the interplay between the writer and his milieu when he noted that: "In evolution there are always two vast fundamental forces; one, the inner, which propels; the other, the outer, which adapts and checks. One forever thrusts toward new forms, the other forever moulds, conserves, adapts, reproduces. . . . The force that flowers is the individual, that which checks and moulds is environment."[17] But in their reaction against the prevalent "great man" school of historical and critical writing, most evolutionary critics tended to emphasize the outer force. Symonds reflected this tendency when he wrote, "The Evolutionist differs from previous students mainly in this, that he regards the totality of the phenomena presented as something necessitated by conditions to which the prime agents in the process, Marlowe or even Shakespeare, were subordinated."[18] In short, evolutionary criticism posited a literature of law, not men.

The evolutionary critics believed that criticism had reached a high point in the modern period. Perhaps the most influential depiction of the advance of criticism was that of Symonds, who viewed the critic as progressively judge, showman, and scientist, or, in another context, as classicist, romanticist, and scientist.[19] Whatever tags they applied to earlier criticism, however, all evolutionary critics used the term scientific to designate the modern critic who, like the scientist, sought a truthful description of the phenomenon under study, a description which precluded exhibitionism and judgment. Howells cautioned that the function of the modern critic was "to classify and analyze the fruits of the human mind very much as the naturalist classifies the objects of his study, rather than to praise or blame them,"[20] while Perry suggested that "it is a question whether praise and blame, admiration and contempt, have anything whatsoever to do with literary history. Our sole aim should be to know."[21] In practice, however, despite Dowden's early and influential call for historical relativism in criticism,[22] most evolutionary critics did apply evaluative standards. They believed that literature progressed as the whole of life progressed, and that the best work of art was therefore almost always that which most closely mirrored the social and intellectual life of its time. In other words, literature was not only describable in terms of its close relation to life, but could also be judged on the basis of its varying degree of reflection of that life. It was this characteristic of evolutionary criticism which made most American evolutionary critics such staunch supporters of realism during the literary controversies of the 1880s and 1890s.

Nevertheless, in theory the scientific critic was distinguished by a willingness to discard judgment and to view literature as a historical process. William Morton Payne called such a critic a "natural historian" of literature and described him as one who

endeavors primarily to account for the work, to view it with reference to the conditions that have attended its production, to consider it, sometimes as a natural development in an established line, sometimes as the expression of a new tendency born of a changed environment or a fresh impulse given the human intellect. . . . He looks before and after, and views literary productions as members of a system rather than as sporadic appearances, as links in a causal chain rather than as isolated phenomena.[23]

Scientific criticism, Payne concluded, is that "controlled by the doctrine of evolution as a guiding principle."[24]

The comparative method, which Posnett characterized as "the great glory" of nineteenth-century thought,[25] was one of the primary tools of the evolutionary critic as well as the evolutionary scientist. It was Darwin's ability to note the similarities and dissimilarities among a large number of species of various areas which had led to his great discovery. Payne indicated the pervasiveness of the association of the comparative method with evolutionary criticism when he claimed that "The study of literature in the evolutionary sense tends more and more to become a comparative study. Just as the geological series of deposits, confused or abruptly broken off in one country, may be found continued elsewhere, so some line of development among the *genres* of literature, clear up to a certain point in the product of one nation, may from that point on be better traced by transferring the scrutiny to some other field."[26]

A possible approach to the understanding and evaluation of evolutionary criticism is to adopt Payne's critical dictum that the critic must look "before and after." Like many literary movements, evolutionary criticism began in reaction, in this case reaction against the supposed subjectivism and absolutism of the criticism of the previous age. It wished to replace personal willfulness and outworn conventions with the law of evolution, an undertaking which to many in the generation after Darwin appeared to be necessary for the attainment of truth in all phases of life. Of course, in their enthusiasm most evolutionary critics went too far, particularly in their atttempts to find biological analogues in literature, in the rigid determinism of their conception of literary change, and in their diminution of the aesthetic evaluative functions of the critic. But looking "after" as well as "before," one can see that the movement was part of a larger reorientation in man's examination of his cultural past, and that it served as a now discarded prelude to much that is accepted and valued in modern criticism and research. It confirmed, for example, the beliefs that discernible change is a major condition of literary history, that an understanding of the life and conventions of a particular age is important and necessary for the understanding of works written during that age, and that comparative studies are a significant contribution to literary research. As in almost every aspect of thought it touched, the theory of evolution aided in the modification of our ideas—in this instance, those concerning the nature and the proper study of literature.

8

Hamlin Garland and Stephen Crane: The Naturalist as Romantic Individualist

M OST CRITICS of American literature no longer feel obliged, as did Bliss Perry in 1912, to preface an examination of the American mind with a defense of the attempt.[1] Now usually accepted are the beliefs that the American experience has been unique and that it has resulted in both a unique intellectual consciousness known as the American mind and a unique literature. What is less certain, however, is the particular nature of the American experience and mind and of their effect upon American literature. One of the most striking common denominators in otherwise often diverse interpretations of the American mind is that of romantic individualism—that is, a pervasive and widespread faith in the validity of the individual experience and mind as a source of knowledge and a guide to action. It is true, of course, that this romantic individualism has never lacked criticism. But its tenacious strength in spite of frequently valid and forceful attack is itself an indication of the depth of the faith in the individual in American life, whether it be expressed in Jeffersonian liberalism, transcendentalism, or the literary revolt of the twenties.

I would like to examine the nature and scope of romantic individualism in the critical ideas of Hamlin Garland and Stephen Crane. These two writers are often discussed as naturalists and the period in which they flourished is almost always considered primarily as a segment of the European naturalistic movement and its influence and manifestation in America. The Zolaesque experimental method is explained and the use of such "scientific" elements in literature as the force of heredity and environment is sketched. All this, of course, is pertinent and necessary. But it is also necessary to indicate that the early American naturalists were very much nineteenth-century Americans and that much in their work and ideas which makes them square pegs in the round hole of such a "standard" definition of naturalism as "pessimistic determinism" may be caused by their absorption of nineteenth-century American ideas. For though Garland and Crane are usually (and rightfully) considered to be among the earliest representatives of American literary naturalism, I wish to point out in addition—not that they were at heart Jeffersonians, transcendentalists, or anticipators of the twenties—but rather that they too, each in his own way, consciously and unconsciously, were part of the broad current which is the stream of American romantic individualism.

In this introduction to *Crumbling Idols,* Hamlin Garland noted the twofold purpose of the work: "to weaken the hold of conventionalism upon the youthful artist" and "to be constructive, by its statement and insistent restatement that American art, to be enduring and worthy, must be original and creative, not imitative."[2] Both of these purposes were in-

trinsically linked to the evolutionary interpretation of literature Garland had derived during his early years in Boston.
During those years (1884–87) he had immersed himself first
in the works of Taine and Herbert Spencer and later in those
of Edward Dowden, H. M. Posnett, William Dean Howells,
and Thomas Sergeant Perry. From Taine he accepted a belief
that literature was conditioned by time and place. From
Spencer, the source of much of his thought, Garland formulated a conception of literature as a dynamic phenomenon
closely related to the physical and social evolutionary progress from incoherent homogeneity to coherent heterogeneity. With the aid of H. M. Posnett's *Comparative Literature* he
then combined these two ideas into an evolutionary critical
system. Literature was required to keep pace with evolutionary progress by mirroring the intense social and individual
differences which the progress from homogeneity to heterogeneity had caused. He concluded that the local colorist was
the only writer capable of capturing contemporary social and
individual complexity, since he alone worked in close enough
detail with an area he knew intimately.

This "dynamic concept of art"—that is, the idea that art
must reflect an ever-changing world—Garland first stated in
an unpublished series of lectures, "The Evolution of American Thought," and repeated again and again in *Crumbling
Idols.* "Life is always changing," he wrote, "and literature
changes with it. It never decays; it changes" (77). The rela-
tivist position in artistic creation and criticism was that art is
not a matter of the imitation or use of the great works or ideas
of the past, but that "life is the model."

Garland, then, conceived of literature as his contemporar-
ies in American philosophy, the pragmatists—also founding
their system upon evolutionary thought—conceived of
ideas.[3] Just as ideas were not absolute because they must

work in the world and the world is ever changing, so art has no absolutes, but must reflect and interpret an ever-changing world by means of new material and new forms. And just as William James's pragmatism sets up a pluralistic universe in which the individual is the source of truth, so Garland conceived of artistic truth as pluralistic and as centered in the individual artist.

Garland derived this emphasis on impressionistic artistic truth from his reading of Véron's *Aesthetics* shortly after he had formulated his evolutionary critical system. In his extensively marked and annotated copy of Véron he wrote on the first page of the Introduction: "This book influenced me more than any other work on art. It entered into all I thought and spoke and read for many years after it fell into my hands about 1886."[4] Véron's critical ideas appealed to Garland because they were in a number of ways parallel to those he himself had just formulated. In his opposition to the French Academy, Véron, who was also the author of *La supériorité des arts modernes sur les arts anciens,* was much in step with the contemporary ideas which had influenced Garland. He too claimed to be using science as the basis for his study, and he too demanded that the artist deal with life about him, since evolution "must give birth to new forms of art appropriate to the new forms of civilization."[5] But whereas Garland had required that local color be the means by which the artist keep pace with evolution, Véron required a form of impressionism. "There are but three ways open to art," he wrote, "the imitation of previous forms of art; the realistic imitation of actual things; the manifestation of individual impressions." Of these three forms of art, Véron argued that only the last deserved the name, for "the determinant and essential constituent of art, is the personality of the artist."[6] But it should be emphasized that Véron's impressionism was restricted and controlled by his insistence that art be anchored in observed fact: "TRUTH and PERSONALITY: These are the alpha and omega of art formulas; *truth* as to facts, and the *personality* of the artist."[7]

Here was a system which shared two characteristics of Garland's own belief. It stressed the necessity for art to represent change, and it required that this be done through the expression of individual personality, the most important product of evolutionary progress from homogeneity to heterogeneity. Garland was sufficiently impressed by Véron's ideas to begin using them almost immediately. So, for example, in noting a talk with his artist friend John Enneking in early 1887, Garland described Enneking's artistic principles in terms of Véron's three kinds of art. Enneking had initially been "conventional" and had "sought the ideal," Garland noted. He had then turned to nature in an attempt to depict it "absolutely as it was." His third and final stage was comparable to Véron's personal impression of observed fact. "He now paints the effect of a scene. That is, he gives us the natural as it affects him."[8]

Garland had little difficulty placing Véron within his evolutionary critical system, since an individual response to observed fact was but another way, to Garland, of stating the idea of local color and all its implications for American literature. For the only literature which could reflect truthfully the life of a particular time and place was that produced by the individual artist, unshackled by rules and conventions, working in close harmony to that life. Garland wrote in *Crumbling Idols:*

Art, I must insist, is an individual thing,—the question of one man facing certain facts and telling his individual relations to them. His first care must be to present his own concept. This is, I believe, the essence of veritism: "Write of those things of which you know most, and for which you care most. By so doing you will be true to yourself, true to your locality, and true to your time." (35)

But as Garland pointed out in *Crumbling Idols,* "The sun of truth strikes each part of the earth at a little different angle" (22). As truth is relative in time because of evolutionary change, so it is relative in place owing to the product of that change, the increased social complexity and heightened individuality which have resulted from evolutionary progress. The impressionist or veritist reflecting the life around him cannot help being a local colorist, since by his reference to nature he must needs represent the uniqueness of his particular area. In *Crumbling Idols* Garland stated an aesthetic system in which evolutionary ideas served as the intellectual foundation, impressionism as the artistic method advocated, and local color as the end product in the various arts.

Throughout *Crumbling Idols* Garland used *impressionism* and *veritism* interchangeably. For example, he defined the two in almost exactly similar terms. Impressionism was "the statement of one's own individual perception of life and nature, guided by devotion to truth" (50); while "This *theory* of the veritist is, after all, a statement of his passion for truth and for individual expression" (21). He appears to have derived the coined word *veritism* as an antonym for *effectism,* Valdés's term (popularized by Howells) for the sensational in literature. In an early article in Ibsen, Garland praised Ibsen's handling of character because it followed "the general principle of verity first and effect afterwards,"[9] and later in the same discussion he used the word *veritist* for the first time. But for Garland, "true" art was primarily the product of an individual response to observed fact, and the term *veritist* soon received the impressionistic cast with which it is used in *Crumbling Idols.*

Far from being the awkward yawp of a confused naturalist (as it usually has been considered), *Crumbling Idols* embodies a coherent aesthetic system. Central to this system—and the emotional center of reference in all of Garland's thought— was the right and need of the individual to be free. The artist must be freed from past and present literary masters in order that he may perceive for himself the truth of his own locality and thereby keep literature in step with evolutionary pro- gress. As Emerson had attempted to free the American schol- ar from that which prevented him from perceiving truth for himself and had called for men of letters to throw off the domination of Europe, so Garland called upon the young writer of the West to interpret life for himself and cast off his subservience to the East. And even Emerson and Whit- man—those fountainheads of American radical individual- ism—would not have stated the doctrine of faith in the indi- vidual artist more vigorously than Garland at the close of *Crumbling Idols:*

Rise, O young man and woman of America! Stand erect! Face the future with a song on your lips and the light of a broader day in your eyes. Turn your back on the past, not in scorn, but in justice to the future. Cease trying to be correct, and become creative. This is our day. The past is not vital. . . . To know Shakespeare is good. To know your fellow men is better. All that Shakespeare knew of human life, you may know, but not at second hand, not through Shakespeare, not through the eyes of the dead, but at first hand. (190–91)[10]

Until some twenty years ago it was customary to begin any consideration of Stephen Crane with an account of the criti- cal neglect of his work. This complaint is no longer justified, for there has been in recent decades much critical interest in both Crane's biography and his work. From the initial treatment of Crane as an inexplicable genius, as a literary "natural," there has evolved a conception of him as a conscious and subtle craftsman and artist. From being considered as a bright but short-lived and uninfluential meteor in the literary firmament, he is now thought, somewhat exaggeratedly to be sure, to have innovated the "two main technical movements of modern fiction—realism and symbolism."[11]

My concern here, however, is not with the meaning or technique of Crane's writing, but rather with the quality of mind and literary self-confidence which led him to that writing. This self-confidence took two literary forms—a choice of material which would shock, as in *Maggie* (1893); and a willingness to trust his imagination in dealing with material about which he knew little, as in *The Red Badge of Courage* (1895). The story of a prostitute who was both a product and a victim of her environment was perhaps not as contemporaneously shocking as it was once thought to be, but to Crane, a young and comparatively unread writer, it appeared so.[12] He inscribed several copies of *Maggie* with the admonition that "It is inevitable that you will be greatly shocked by the book but continue, please, with all possible courage, to the end."[13] A serious author who will knowingly shock his readers is an author confident of the correctness of his vision of life, despite its being out of joint with conventional morality. And an author who will—as Crane did in *The Red Badge*—trust his imaginative conception of war and of its effects on men is just as confident of the validity of his personal vision.

One reason for Crane's self-confidence suggests itself immediately. Both *Maggie* and *The Red Badge* were written before Crane was twenty-three. In Crane's case, however, the self-confidence of a youthful and temperamentally cocky personality was reinforced and given an explicit rhetoric by the acceptance of an impressionistic critical doctrine. A clue to the source of this doctrine lies in Crane's lifelong sense of debt toward Hamlin Garland and William Dean Howells. This sense of debt was undoubtedly derived in part from Garland's and Howells's early aiding and championing of Crane. But it also derived, it appears, from Crane's early adoption and use of a particular critical idea of Garland's and Howells's.

In 1891, when Crane was nineteen and had as yet written little, he spent the summer helping his brother report New Jersey shore news for the *New York Tribune*. One of his assignments was to cover a series of "Lecture Studies in American Literature and Expressive Art" which Hamlin Garland was giving at the Avon-by-the-Sea Seaside Assembly.[14] Garland, at this time, was an enthusiastic advocate of impressionism in painting and literature and was formulating and writing the essays which would comprise *Crumbling Idols*. On August 17, Garland gave a lecture on Howells which Crane reported for the *Tribune*. Garland, in discussing Howells's work and ideas, placed him squarely in his own evolutionary, impressionistic critical system. Howells, Crane reported Garland, believed in "'the progress of ideals, the relative in art.'" He therefore "'does not insist upon any special material, but only that the novelist be true to himself and to things as he sees them.'"[15] On the surface, it would appear that these remarks would make little impression on a listener. But Crane not only heard them, he reported them. Moreover, he immediately became acquainted with Garland and spent some time with him at Avon that summer and the next, when Garland again gave a lecture series and Crane again reported shore news.

In 1895 Crane inscribed a copy of *The Red Badge* to Howells as a token of the "veneration and gratitude of Stephen Crane for many things he has learned of the common man and, above all, for a certain readjustment of his point of view vic-

toriously concluded some time in 1892."[16] About a year earlier he had written in a letter that in 1892 he had renounced
the "clever school in literature" and had "developed all alone
a little creed of art which I thought was a good one. Later I
discovered that my creed was identical with the one of
Howells and Garland."[17] The important elements in these
two statements of literary indebtedness are Crane's realization of a debt to Howells and his further realization of the
similarity of his "little creed" with the critical ideas of Garland and Howells. Whether Crane discovered his creed "all
alone" and merely received confirmation from Garland and
Howells, or whether he "victoriously concluded" his acceptance of the creed after being introduced to it by Garland's
statement of Howells's belief, is perhaps not too important.
Important, rather, is Crane's derivation in 1892 of a concept
of personal honesty and vision similar to both Garland's
idea—which Garland saw exemplified in Howells—that
" 'the novelist [must] be true to himself and to things as he
sees them' " and Howells's own statement that the novelist
should above all "remember that there is no greatness, no
beauty, which does not come from truth to your own knowledge of things."[18] Crane distinctly parallels these statements
in several of his sparsely recorded critical remarks. In 1896,
for example, he wrote: "I had no other purpose in writing
'Maggie' than to show people to people as they seem to me. If
that be evil, make the most of it,"[19] Earlier that year he had
stated this idea even more elaborately: "I understand that a
man is born into the world with his own pair of eyes, and he is
not at all responsible for his vision—he is merely responsible
for his quality of personal honesty."[20]

Crane, then, entered the literary arena armed with a powerful weapon—a belief in the primacy of his personal vision.
On a superficial level, this faith led him to exploit and defend

the unconventional and forbidden in *Maggie,* confident of the validity of showing "people to people as they seem to me." On a level of greater depth and significance, his faith in his own vision led him to exploit his inner eye, his imaginative conception of war and its effects. In both, Crane—like Garland—was revealing an acceptance of the strain of romantic individualism which demands that the artist above all be independent and self-reliant, that he be confident that within himself lies the touchstone of artistic truth.

9

Frank Norris's Definition
of Naturalism

FRANK NORRIS'S DEFINITION of naturalism is important because an understanding of his use of the term may help to explain both his own practice of fiction and the more general American reaction to Zolaesque literary principles. My reason for reintroducing the much-debated question of Norris's definition is that I believe new light can be shed on the subject by the examination of not only his well-known "A Plea for Romantic Fiction," but also his lesser-known "Zola as a Romantic Writer" and his relatively unknown "Weekly Letter" in the *Chicago American* of August 3, 1901.[1]

Norris placed realism, romanticism, and naturalism in a dialectic, in which realism and romanticism were opposing forces, and naturalism was transcending synthesis. Realism, to Norris, was the literature of the normal and representative, "the smaller details of every-day life, things that are likely to happen between lunch and supper."[2] Moreover, realism does not probe the inner reaches of life; it "notes only the surface of things."[3] Howells is Norris's archetype of the realistic writer. Romanticism differs from realism both in its concern for "variations from the type of normal life,"[4] and in its desire to penetrate beneath the surface of experience and derive large generalizations on the nature of life. Romanticism explores "the unplumbed depths of the human heart, and the mystery of sex, and the problems of life, and the black, unsearched penetralia of the soul of man."[5] To Norris "the greatest of all modern romanticists" is Hugo.[6]

Now what of naturalism? Although Norris at times called Zola a romanticist, it is clear that he intended in that designation to emphasize Zola's lack of affinity to Howellsian realism rather than to eliminate naturalism as a distinctive descriptive term.[7] Naturalism, as conceived by Norris, resolved the conflict between realism and romanticism by selecting the best from these two modes and by adding one constituent ignored by both. In his "Weekly Letter" to the *Chicago American* of August 3, 1901, he partially described this synthesis. He began with a distinction between Accuracy and Truth. Accuracy is fidelity to particular detail; Truth is fidelity to the generalization applicable to a large body of experience. Since a novel may therefore be accurate in its depiction of a segment of life and yet be untrue, Norris inquired what is the source of truth in fiction, if a literal transcription of life itself is inadequate. He began to find his way out of this dilemma when he asked:

It is permissible to say that Accuracy is realism and Truth romanticism? I am not so sure, but I feel that we come close to a solution here. The divisions seem natural and intended. It is not difficult to be accurate, but it is monstrously difficult to be True; at best the romanticists can only aim at it, while on the other hand, mere accuracy as an easily obtainable result is for that reason less worthy.[8]

Norris then asked:

Does Truth after all "lie in the middle"? And what school, then, is midway between the Realists and Romanticists, taking the best from each? Is it not the school of Naturalism, which strives hard for accuracy and truth? The nigger is out of the fence at last, but must it not be admitted that the author of *La Débâcle* (not the author of *La Terre* and *Fécondité*)[9] is up to the present stage of literary development the most adequate, the most satisfactory, the most just of them all?[10]

Naturalism, in short, abstracts the best from realism and romanticism—detailed accuracy and philosophical depth. In addition, naturalism differs from both modes in one important characteristic of its subject matter. As Norris explained in his *Wave* essay on "Zola as a Romantic Writer":

That Zola's work is not purely romantic as was Hugo's lies chiefly in the choice of Milieu. These great, terrible dramas no longer happen among the personnel of a feudal and Renaissance nobility, those who are in the fore-front of the marching world, but among the lower—almost the lowest—classes; those who have been thrust or wrenched from the ranks, who are falling by the roadway. This is not romanticism—this drama of the people, working itself out in blood and ordure. It is not realism. It is a school by itself, unique, somber, powerful beyond words. It is naturalism.[11]

What is particularly absorbing in this definition is that it is limited entirely to subject matter and method. It does not mention materialistic determinism or any other philosophical idea, and thus differs from the philosophical orientation both of Zola's discussions of naturalism and of those by modern critics of the movement.[12] Norris conceived of naturalism as a fictional mode which illustrated some fundamental truth of life within a detailed presentation of the sensational and low. Unlike Zola, however, he did not specify the exact nature of the truth to be depicted, and it is clear that he believed Hugo's "truth" as naturalistic as Zola's. With Norris's definition in mind, then, we can perhaps understand his remark to Isaac Marcosson that *The Octopus* was going to be a return to the "style" of *McTeague*—"straight naturalism."[13] Although the early novel is consciously deterministic in its treatment of human action and the later one dramatizes a complex intermingling of free will and determinism, this contradiction is nonexistent within the philosophical vacuum of Norris's definition.

Norris's definition, however, is not only significant for his own fictional practice. It also clarifies some fundamental characteristics of the naturalistic movement in America. It suggests that for many Americans influenced by European naturalistic currents, the naturalistic mode involved primarily the contemporary, low, and sensational, which was elaborately documented within a large thematic framework. The writer might give his work a philosophical center—indeed, the naturalistic mode encouraged such a practice. But the core ideas or values present in particular works tended to be strikingly diverse from author to author, as each writer approached his material from an individual direction rather than from the direction of an ideological school. American naturalism, in other words, has been largely a movement characterized by similarities in material and method, not by philosophical coherence. And perhaps this very absence of a philosophical center to the movement has been one of the primary reasons for its continuing strength in this country, unlike its decline in Europe. For writers as different as Dreiser and Crane, or Farrell and Faulkner, have responded to the

exciting possibilities of a combination of romantic grandiose-
ness, detailed verisimilitude, and didactic sensationalism,
and yet, like Norris, have been able to shape these possibilities into works expressing most of all their own distinctive
temperaments.

10

The Significance of
Frank Norris's Literary Criticism

ALTHOUGH FRANK NORRIS'S critical essays are poorly written, repetitious, and occasionally plain silly, they nevertheless contain a coherent critical attitude of some importance. Norris is not often discussed as a writer capable of intellectual consistency in any matter. Most critics have approached him as did Franklin Walker in his biography of Norris. In that work Walker stressed Norris's boyish enthusiasm and his code of "feeling" raised above "thought."[1] Walker implied by this emphasis that Norris was not a systematic thinker and that it would be futile to search for a consistent intellectual position in his fiction or criticism. But Walker's characterization of Norris is misleading for two reasons. A writer under thirty does not have to appear solemn to think seriously. And the rejection of "thought" for "feeling" is itself capable of expansion into an elaborate intellectual position. Because Norris advised others to feel does not mean that his advice was not reasoned. Indeed, in the history of man much thought has been devoted to the creation of anti-intellectual philosophies.

At the heart of the unified and coherent system of ideas underlying Norris's criticism is a primitivistic anti-intellectualism.[2] One method of describing this system is to adopt as convenient counter words the key terms in Norris's cry that life is better than literature. Superficially, he meant by this statement that first-hand experience ("life") is better than second-hand experience ("literature"). But when the terms are placed in the context of Norris's critical essays, one realizes that they are his inadequate symbols for two rich and opposing clusters of ideas and values. I therefore use "life" and "literature" both with a recognition of their deficiencies as generally viable critical terminology and with an appreciation of their usefulness and appropriateness when analysing Norris's critical ideas.

To Norris, "life" included the emotions and the instincts. It incorporated both the world of nature (the outdoors and the country) and the kind of life which Norris believed "natural" (the life of passion and violence, and the life of the low and fallen) because such life was closest to the primitive in man and furthest from the cultivated. "Literature," on the other hand, included thought, culture, overeducation, refinement, and excessive spirituality. "Life" was dominated by connotations of masculinity, naturalness, and strength; "literature" by suggestions of effeminancy, artificiality, and weakness. "Life" was the source of good art—from it sprang art which moved and led men—whereas from "literature" came imitative and affected art, written entirely for money or for the approval of a cult, or because the artist was unfortunate or unknowing enough to overrefine his temperament and to neglect the crude, raw, often violent world of action and affairs—the world of men and of nature. Norris thus made the emotional and instinctive the key to both the method and the material of fiction, since he encouraged writers to respond to a world of nonintellectuality with their own un-taught vision.

Although primitivistic anti-intellectualism has a long histo-ry in American literature, Norris's expression of it differs from that of earlier and later writers with generally similar values. The central polarity in such writers as Hawthorne and Thoreau or Steinbeck and Faulkner is not only between the emotional-instinctive and the intellectual, but also, and more far-reaching, between the organicism of nature and the mechanization of science and industrialism. Norris, howev-er, applauds the advances of modern industrialism. He views scientific mechanization as no threat to man, but rather as a means toward universal betterment, so long as the abuses of an uncontrolled industrialism are corrected. Norris, then, does not participate in the nature-machine conflict of earlier and later romantic writers. Rather, he substitutes for the ma-chine the contemporary aesthetic movement, and—with some justice—views that movement as the major threat to the primitive values present in his conception of "life." He is thus caught up not so much in the realism-romanticism con-troversy of the nineties as in that decade's conflict between a decadent aestheticism and an emerging school of manliness, adventure, and the outdoors.

This second, more pertinent conflict is more clearly de-fined in England than in America, since our own aesthetic movement was primarily a weak imitation of English and French currents. In England, however, a genuine, vicious, and much publicized battle was fought between the school of Wilde, Beardsley, and the *Yellow Book* and that of Henley, Kipling, and Stevenson.[3] This struggle reached a climax in the trial of Wilde in 1895 and the apparent victory of the forces of "decency," virility, and moral art. But its ramifica-tions continued into the early years of the new century, kept alive in part by the vogue of Bohemianism and by the discussion of Max Nordau's thesis in *Degeneration* that almost all modern art was degenerate.[4]

To Norris, therefore, as late as 1902 "literature" was characterized by the stylistics of Pater, by the "spirituality" of Ruskin, and most of all by Wilde's doctrine of the superiority of art to nature. "I was a man who stood in symbolic relations to the art and culture of my age," Wilde wrote in *De Profundis*, and one can see a rather twisted application of that statement in Norris's tendency to characterize "literature" in sexual terms as effeminate, with some suggestions of homosexuality. Indeed, much of the emotional force present in Norris's attack on literary style can only be understood in relation to his revulsion from the eroticism and homosexuality associated with Wilde, Beardsley and Huysmans.

In opposition to these figures was the group of writers, led by Henley, whom Jerome Buckley has called the "counter-decadents."[5] This counter movement reached its fulfillment in the work of Kipling. And just as Norris's description of "literature" often seems an epitome of the popular conception of Wilde, so his idea of "life" is intimately related both to the fiction and the aesthetic theory of Kipling. Like Norris, Kipling asserted the intrinsic value of both nature and machine. (The two faiths are strikingly combined in the two halves of *Captains Courageous*—the boy's "education" off the Grand Banks, the father's brilliant railroad journey.) Like Norris, Kipling posited aestheticism as the chief obstacle to the portrayal of "life," and like Norris he located aestheticism in literary centers and in universities. Almost all of Kipling's basic literary theory appears in *The Light That Failed*, which Norris read in the early 1890s. In that novel Dick Heldar, the artist-war correspondent, took part in battles and then painted them in all their violence, brutality, and dirt. He finds, however, that London art dealers and magazine editors want neat, tidy battle scenes, and he is almost led by them into painting pictures of that kind. Maisie, on the other hand, is a sheltered, imitative, innocuous painter concerned primarily with gaining public approval. This contrast, and Dick's frequently expressed contempt for "Art" (always capitalized), supplied Norris with much of the rhetoric of his "life"-"literature" antithesis.

It is not surprising, then, to find a Wilde-Kipling contrast running through Norris's descriptions of "literature" and "life," a contrast sharpened and vitalized by his personal rejection of the minor Bohemian worlds he encountered in San Francisco and New York.[6] Indeed, he tended in his later criticism to establish Kipling-like conflicts between the virile artist and a corrupting city aestheticism.[7] One of the best examples of this tendency, and also of Norris's basic "life"-"literature" antithesis, is his story "Dying Fires," published in 1902.[8]

"Dying Fires" tells of Overbeck, a young man born and raised in the Colfax mining district of the California Sierras. At the age of twenty-one, Overbeck writes a novel—*The Vision of Bunt McBride*—about the teamsters and waitresses, the dance halls and gambling joints of Colfax. It was a good novel, Norris stated, because "young Overbeck had got started right at the very beginning. He had not been influenced by a fetich of his choice till his work was a mere replica of some other writer's. He was not literary. He had not much time for books. He lived in the midst of a strenuous, eager life, a little primal even yet; a life of passions that were often elemental in their simplicity and directness" (114). This combination of elemental material and an unspoiled literary sensibility results in a powerful novel which brings Overbeck a call to New York. There he works in an editorial office and becomes a member of a literary set called "New Bohemia."

It was made up of minor poets [Norris writes], whose opportunity in life was the blank space on a magazine page below the end of an article; of men past their prime, who, because of an occasional story in a second-rate monthly, were considered to have "arrived"; of women who translated novels from the Italian and Hungarian; of decayed dramatists who could advance unimpeachable reasons for the non-production of their plays; of novelists whose books were declined by publishers because of professional jealousy on the part of the "readers." (119)

New Bohemia has its effect on Overbeck. Soon, Norris tells us,

He could talk about "tendencies" and the "influence of reactions." Such and such a writer had a "sense of form," another a "feeling for word effects." He knew all about "tones" and "notes" and "philistinisms." He could tell the difference between an allegory and a simile. . . . An anti climax was the one unforgivable sin under heaven. A mixed metaphor made him wince, and a split infinitive hurt him like a blow. (120)

The New Bohemians encourage him to write another novel, but one quite different from the "sane and healthy animalism" of *The Vision of Bunt McBride*. " 'Art must uplift,' " they tell him:

Ah, the spititual was the great thing. We were here to make the world brighter and better for having lived in it. The passions of a waitress in a railway eatinghouse—how sordid the subject. Dear boy, look for the soul, strive to rise to higher planes! Tread upward; every book should leave a clean taste in the mouth, should tend to make one happier, should elevate, not debase. (122)

He begins a second novel, *Renunciations*, which Norris describes as a "city-bred story, with no fresher atmosphere than that of bought flowers. Its *dramatis personae* were all of the leisure class, operagoers, intriguers, riders of blood horses" (123). (Norris seems to be using Henry James as a model here.) *Renunciations* is a failure, and Overbeck, realizing his mistake, returns to Colfax and attempts to rekindle his creative fires. "But the ashes were cold by now," Norris concludes. "The fire that the gods had allowed him to snatch . . . had been stamped out beneath the feet of minor and dilettante poets, and now the gods guarded close the brands that yet remained on the altars" (126–27).

"Dying Fires" is thus almost an allegory of Norris's beliefs about "life" and "literature," of his conviction that the best fiction derives from an untutored vision of the raw and violent in experience. But now one comes to a vital paradox in Norris's critical thought, one hinted at in "Dying Fires" when Norris noted of Overbeck's first novel that despite its power it revealed a "lack of knowledge of his tools" because of Overbeck's literary inexperience. For Norris combined with his primitivistic ideas an equally confirmed faith in what he called "the mechanics of fiction"—that is, a belief that the form and technique of fiction have certain rules, "tricks," and procedures which can not only be described, but which can also be taught, and which must be acquired through arduous discipline and application. In other words, as far as the form of the novel is concerned, Norris attacked the instinctive, the emotional, the natural. He believed that fictional form is an intellectual problem in selection and organization for the achievement of plausibility, effect, and theme, and that there are few substitutes for a considered and painstak-

ing intellectual solution. Commenting in 1901 on a proposed
school of novel writing, Norris wrote:

Some certain people—foolish people—often say: "Teach people
how to write novels! It must be born in you. There is no other way."
I do not believe this. Nobody is born with the ability to write fiction. The greatest writers have to learn it all for themselves. If they
taught themselves they could to a very large extent teach others. It
is not at all impossible of belief that the fundamentals of construction in fiction could be in a manner codified, formulized and stud-
ied with as much good results as the fundamentals of any other of
the professions.
    All other of the fine arts demand preparatory courses of train-
ing—sculpture, painting, music, acting, architecture, and the like.
Why should fiction be the one—the only one—to be ignored? Be
well assured of this: The construction of a novel is as much of an exact science as the construction of a temple or a sonnet. The laws and
rules of this construction have never been adequately formulated,
but they exist.[9]

It is upon this fundamental duality, then, that Norris's
critical system rests—"life, not literature" as far as theme
and content are concerned, but "literature, not life" as far as
form is concerned. Of the two, he gave the first priority.
Without "life" as a foundation, no amount of technical training would benefit a writer. The best novelist, however, was
he who was primitivistic in content and theme, sophisticated
in form.

This duality in Norris's critical ideas anticipates and clarifies a major development in the American novel. There had always been a strong current of primitivistic anti-intellectualism
in nineteenth-century American fiction, from Leatherstocking baiting the scientist Obed Bat in *The Prairie* to Huck Finn
deciding to obey his heart rather than his conscience. This

faith in the life of action, instinct, and emotion continues as a
central force in the modern American novel, as in the work of
Faulkner, Hemingway, and Steinbeck. There is little doubt
that it is one of our distinctive national faiths.[10] The importance of Norris's criticism is not only that he is our earliest
critic to found an aesthetic of the novel upon this faith, but
also that he combines with his primitivism a demand that the
novel be cultivated as an art form, and thereby represents a
major bridge between the ungainly novels of a Cooper or
Twain and the virtuoso techniques of a Hemingway or Faulkner. Much of our best modern fiction thus answers Norris's
key demands, since it often combines an intense thematic
primitivism with a striking facility in the manipulation of
point of view, time, scene, and symbol. In short, the sophisticated primitivism which Norris required is a primary characteristic of twentieth-century American fiction. It is found
both among our established novelists and among the more
exciting postwar writers, such as Mailer, Bellow, and Styron.
Whatever the crudities, the lapses, and the journalistic short-
cuts of Norris's criticism, then, that criticism is important not
only for the obvious reasons that it tells us much about Norris's own fictional practice and that it clarifies many of the literary issues of the time. His criticism is significant primarily
because it increases our understanding of some of the most
basic and seemingly most enduring characteristics of American fiction.

11

The Ethical Unity of
The Rise of Silas Lapham

CRITICS OF HOWELLS'S *The Rise of Silas Lapham* have usually examined its subplot as an excrescence arising from a need to satisfy the popular demand for a romantic entanglement, as a digressive attack on the sentimental self-sacrifice of the "Tears, Idle Tears" variety, or as an overexpansion of the comedy of manners strain in the novel. Each of these points of view has a certain validity. But it is also true that the subplot and main plot have fundamentally similar themes, and that an examination of the thematic function of the subplot will elucidate both the ethical core of the novel and the relationship of that core to a prominent theme in Howells's later economic novels.[1]

The main plot of *The Rise of Silas Lapham* concerns Silas's financial fall and moral rise. It revolves around his business affairs and social aspirations, and it concludes with his decision to sacrifice wealth and position rather than engage in business duplicity. The subplot centers on the triangle of Tom Corey and Irene and Penelope Lapham. Tom is mistakenly believed by all to be in love with Irene. The dilemma caused by his revelation that he loves Penelope is resolved when Irene is informed of the error. Irene then withdraws, leaving Tom and Penelope free to marry.

The dilemma or conflict within the subplot is solved by the use of an "economy of pain" formula.[2] Despite Penelope's willingness to sacrifice herself, Irene must be told of Corey's true sentiments, and Penelope and Corey must be encouraged to fulfill their love. In this way Irene suffers but Penelope and Tom are spared the pain of thwarted love. One rather than three suffers lasting pain. Of the three characters who determine the resolution of the subplot, Lapham realizes instinctively the correct course of action, Mrs. Lapham is helpless and hesitant—this despite her moralizing throughout the novel—and the clergyman Sewell articulates the principle involved and confirms Lapham's choice.

The problem which Silas must solve in the main plot parallels that in the subplot. The three groups who will be affected by his decision are he and his family (Lapham is a participant now as well as an arbiter), Rogers and his family, and the English agents who wish to purchase Lapham's depreciated mill.[3] The crucial point is that the Englishmen are more than mere scoundrels and more than the agents for an "association of rich and charitable people" (325); they also represent society at large. This fact is somewhat obscured in the context of the financial trickery involved in the sale, since the agents are willing to be cheated. But Howells indicated the social implications of the sale when he immediately compared it to the defrauding of municipal governments. In both instances wealth and anonymity encourage dishonesty, and in both instances dishonesty undermines that which is necessary for the maintenance of the common good—effective governments on the one hand, fair play and honest dealings in business affairs on the other. Lapham's refusal to sell therefore ultimately contributes to the well-being of society as a whole.

The thematic similarity in the two plots is that both involve a principle of morality which requires that the individual determine correct action by reference to the common good rather than to an individual need. Within the subplot this principle requires Lapham to choose on the basis of an "economy of pain" formula in which the fewest suffer. Within the main plot it requires him to weigh his own and Rogers's personal needs against the greater need of all men for decency and honesty. His "rise" is posited exactly in these terms, for at one point in the events leading up to his rejection of the Englishmen's offer he reflects quizzically that "It was certainly ridiculous for a man who had once so selfishly consulted his own interests to be stickling now about the rights of others" (330).

The method used to achieve moral insight is also similar in both plots. What is required is the ability to project oneself out of the immediate problem in which the personal, emotionally compelling need or desire is seen out of proportion to the need of the larger unit. In the subplot Mrs. Lapham finds this difficult, and Sewell asks her, " 'What do you think some one else ought to do in your place?' " (240) In the main plot it is no doubt Silas's realization of the honesty that he would ask of other men in a similar situation which aids him in making the same demand of himself. Lastly, as in the subplot, Silas is capable of moral insight, Mrs. Lapham again falters, and Sewell (at the end of the novel) attempts explanations.

One of the functions of the subplot is therefore to "double" the moral theme of the novel, to intensify and clarify it by introducing it within a narrower, more transparent dilemma. The subplot also plays other important roles. Dominating the center of the novel it is solved before the full exposition of

Lapham's business crisis.[4] It occurs, in other words, between Howells's early remark that Lapham "could not rise" (50) to unselfishness in his dealings with Rogers and Lapham's own words at the close which indicate a concern for the "rights of others." The subplot thus contributes to the "education" of Lapham in the correct solution of moral problems. His moral rise is the product of more than a conscience troubled by his earlier treatment of Rogers. It is also the result of his ready absorption of the "economy of pain" formula as a moral guide in the subplot, a formula which he later translates into its exact corollary, the greatest happiness for the greatest number, when he is faced in the main plot with the more difficult problem of the ethical relationship of the individual to society. To sum up, the subplot of *The Rise of Silas Lapham* serves the functions of doubling the statement of the novel's theme, of foreshadowing the moral principle governing the main plot, and of introducing Lapham to the correct solution of moral problems.[5]

It is possible, at this point, to suggest that the ethical core of the novel can be described as utilitarianism (as interpreted by John Stuart Mill), since both plots dramatize a moral principle in which the correct action is that which results in the greatest happiness for the greatest number. I do not wish to intimate that Howells consciously adopted the ethical ideas of Mill. Rather, I believe that the similarity between Mill's utilitarianism and the ethical principles of *The Rise of Silas Lapham* is probably the result of parallel attempts to introduce the ethical teachings of Christ within social contexts and yet avoid supernatural sanctions. Howells's emerging Christian socialism in the late 1880s is well known,[6] and Mill wrote:

I must again repeat . . . that the happiness which forms the utilitarian standard of what is right in conduct, is not the agent's own happiness, but that of all concerned. . . . In the golden rule of Jesus of Nazareth, we read the complete spirit of the ethics of utility. To do as you would be done by, and to love your neighbor as yourself, constitute the ideal perfection of utilitarian morality.[7]

That Howells was conscious of the applicability of the Golden Rule to the theme of *The Rise of Silas Lapham* is clear, I believe, from his ironic use of it in connection with Rogers. When Rogers senses that Lapham may reject the Englishmen's offer, his appeal to Lapham is based on the premise that

In our dealings with each other we should be guided by the Golden Rule, as I was saying to Mrs. Lapham before you came in. I told her that if I knew myself, I should in your place consider the circumstances of a man in mine, who had honorably endeavored to discharge his obligations to me, and had patiently borne my undeserved suspicions. I should consider that man's family, I told Mrs. Lapham. (327)

But Lapham's answer is the response of a man who is aware of the sophistry of a narrow use of the Golden Rule and who recognizes the necessity for the consideration of a wider range of obligation that individual need. " 'Did you tell her,' " he asks Rogers, " 'that if I went in with you and those fellows, I should be robbing the people who trusted them?' " (327)

There is a twofold advantage in viewing the main and subplots of *The Rise of Silas Lapham* as controlled by a similar conception of moral behavior. First, the novel takes on a thematic unity and structural symmetry. It is within a single moral system, for example, that the apparent conflict between the attack on self-sacrifice in the subplot and Lapham's self-sacrifice in the main plot is reconciled. Penelope's self-sacrifice would diminish the sum total of happiness of those affected by her action, and therefore is wrong; Silas's self-sacrifice increases the happiness of mankind collectively, and therefore is right.[8] Secondly, the theme of the novel anticipates Howells's acceptance of Tolstoy's ethical ideals within the next few years and helps explain his response to those ideals once he encountered them. For in the two plots of *The Rise of Silas Lapham* Howells had already begun working out a belief that man must rise above himself and view life, as, he later explained, Tolstoy had taught him to view life, "not as a chase of a forever impossible personal happiness, but as a field for endeavor toward the happiness of the whole human family."[9] The conviction that man's primary commitment is to mankind was to be one of the themes which Howells emphasized in the series of novels from *Annie Kilburn* (1888) to *A Traveller from Altruria* (1894). In *The Rise of Silas Lapham* that theme appears in a less obvious social context (Howells had to strain for the connection between the English agents and society) and—more importantly—as an obligation which the average individual can grasp and fulfill. His novels during the years following the Haymarket crisis were to examine the theme of man's duty to his fellow men more intensively but less hopefully.

12

Hamlin Garland's 1891 *Main-Travelled Roads*: Local Color as Art

H AMLIN GARLAND WAS born in a narrow upland valley (a "coolly") near West Salem, Wisconsin, on September 14, 1860. His father was a farmer, and Garland spent his youth as a farm boy in western Wisconsin and in northeastern Iowa, near Osage. From 1876 to 1881 he worked on the family farm from spring to fall and attended the Cedar Valley Seminary in Osage during the winter. ("Seminary" was a western name for any school offering advanced education.) Garland's graduation in 1881 coincided with his father's decision to resettle his family on new land in South Dakota. But Garland himself was dissatisfied with farming as a way of life. Instead of joining his family, he spent three miscellaneous years in the West as a school teacher, carpenter, and South Dakota land claimant. In October, 1884, he sold his Dakota claim and moved to Boston in order to prepare himself for a career as a teacher of literature.

This recital of the bare facts of Garland's youth casts considerable light on the subject matter of *Main-Travelled Roads*. Garland's experiences as a farm boy are the source of his inti-

mate knowledge of the details of farm life and of his awareness that the seasonal cycle of planting and harvest is the
principal reality of a farm existence. His biography also suggests the source and location of the three "matters" of his
middle border fictional world. Settled primarily in the two
decades following the Civil War, the middle border was the
area between the older states of the Northwest Territory
(Ohio, Indiana, Illinois) and the last frontier of the Rocky
Mountains. To Garland, the middle border was specifically
the high valleys of western Wisconsin ("Up the Coulé" and
"The Return of a Private"), the wheat and stock farms of
Iowa ("A Branch-Road," "Under the Lion's Paw," and
"Mrs. Ripley's Trip"), and the plains of Dakota ("Among
the Corn-Rows"). Most of his middle border stories are set in
Iowa, since his years as an Iowa farm boy and seminarian
were the principal sources of his knowledge of western farm
and town life.

Garland's early years influenced the stories of *Main-
Travelled Roads* in other important ways. As he came of age in
Iowa, he experienced both the backbreaking, mind-numbing
labor of an unmechanized and understaffed western farm
and the world of the mind and spirit which he was encountering at the seminary. By the time he graduated, he had come
to associate the first kind of life with his father and with farming and the second with the city, particularly with the cities of
the East, from which all culture came. His first independent
act, therefore, was to leave his father and farming, and his
second was to make his way to Boston. These two actions
were to constitute the emotional center of Garland's personal
and literary life for over a decade. On the one hand, he had
successfully rebelled against the life of the farm and had escaped to the richer world of the East. On the other, escape
meant desertion—desertion not only of his family, particular-

ly of his overworked and rapidly aging mother, but also of his region and its needs. When Garland came to write his early stories of the middle border, he discovered that the themes of joyous escape and guilty return were intimately associated with his response to his area.

In Boston, Garland soon made a place for himself. After some initial difficulties and hardships, he succeeded in becoming a lecturer and teacher. Various Bostonians who had cultivated him as an interesting western type found that his personal intensity and wideranging "advanced" ideas were compelling in their own right. He became friendly with a large number of minor writers and artists and visited their homes and studios. In mid-1886, he began to write reviews and articles for the high-toned *Boston Evening Transcript*, and a year later he met and interested William Dean Howells, then the foremost American literary personage. He had grown a Van Dyke beard, and with his Inverness cape and slouch hat he was a striking figure in the subdued Boston literary scene of the late 1880s.

During his early years in Boston, Garland was under the spell of the evolutionary philosophy of Herbert Spencer. Guided by Spencer's belief that all life was an evolutionary progress from the simple to the complex, he wrote an ambitious history of American literature. Despite the labor required of him as a teacher and critic, he also began to think of himself as an embryonic writer of fiction. He had been stimulated by the recent work of such midwestern writers as E. W. Howe and Joseph Kirkland, and in part under their influence began a number of middle border short stories and a Dakota novel. But by mid-1887 Garland had been away from Iowa and Wisconsin for many years. It was therefore with the thought of refreshing his memory of western life, as well as seeing his family, that he arranged a trip to the West in the summer of 1887. He would not only visit Ordway, South Dakota, where his family was farming, but also his old homes in Iowa and Wisconsin.

During his trip Garland kept a journal in which he recorded his impressions and ideas. Two recurrent themes appear in these notes—his dismay at the conditions of western life, and his conviction that these conditions were both explainable and remediable. Garland's dismay, of course, was in part the product of his years in Boston. Shabby, dust-filled towns and fly-blown, suffocating farm kitchens were depressingly bleak after the theatres, concerts, and physical comforts of city life. But Garland's shock was also conditioned by his conscious comparison of western life as it was and as it had been traditionally portrayed. In conventional novels and poems about farm life, the independent farmer, "with his simple rusticity and healthful habits," was characterized as "the happiest man in the world."[1] As Garland travelled west, however, he found not the happy yeoman but the Iowa farmer, who, he noted,

has more to irritate him than any other sort of man on earth. The calves, pigs, and horses are as perverse as ugly dispositions can make them. The farmer wears dirty and sticky clothing, goes without bathing, is parched by the wind and burned by the sun. He is a pack-horse who never lays down his load.

No beauty, no music comes into his life. He lives apart from his fellows and all the little courtesies and amenities of life are unknown to him.[2]

Garland's angle of vision in this passage is initially that of the "insider" who knows the truth about farm life and who therefore implicitly despises the bucolic as a literary convention. But he is also an "outsider" who is aware of the rich life, the "beauty," which is both unknown and unavailable to the farmer. This two-fold vision of western life is present in many of the stories of *Main-Travelled Roads*. Occasionally it appears as an awkwardly explicit anti-bucolic statement, as in "Up the Coulé": " 'The poet who writes of milking the cows does it from the hammock, looking on,' Howard soliloquized, as he watched the old man Lewis racing around the filthy yard after one of the young heifers that had kicked over the pail in her agony with the flies and was unwilling to stand still and be eaten alive."[3] But more often, and more effectively, Garland's double angle of vision unobtrusively colors scene after scene in which he depicts the drudgery and sterility of farm life. For example, his choice of detail in the scene just noted—the flies and filth of farmyard milking—represents a conscious reversal of one of the traditional idyllic images of the pastoral.

Garland not only found western town and country life inadequate but also, as I have noted, had an explanation for this condition. Even before coming to Boston he had read Henry George's *Progress and Poverty*, and during his Boston years his belief in George's land theories had deepened. As he viewed the West, therefore, he attributed, as did George, all economic and social deprivation to the evils of land speculation. He commented in his notebook:

As one goes west from Charles City [Iowa], the country changes to a fresher green. There is much open land, richly covered with grasses, a paradise for stock-raisers and yet few make use of it. The houses are mainly hovels, the towns are squalid little affairs and the whole land looks as though blighted by some mysterious curse. And it is—the speculator's curse.

The country, though splendidly fertile, is but sparsely settled, the settlers passing over it for the purpose of getting the free lands beyond. What part of it as is farmed is but scratched over. The enormous productive power of the land is untouched. The settlers

have a crude, rough look, thin, small and dressed illy. They show
that they live apart from the centers of thought.

As one looks at the wretched little farms, the ghastly little towns,
and the splendid sort of a pleasant country lying waste, he ex-
claims, here is the very example of the folly of our land system.[4]

The controlling image in this passage is that of a rich, fertile
land lying vacant because it is owned by speculators who are
waiting for high prices (and therefore large mortgages) while
farmers scratch out a living on less arable but cheaper land
farther west. It is an image which Garland later shaped into
the plot and theme of his most well-known story, "Under the
Lion's Paw." Henry George had argued that land speculation
would be impossible if all land in a specific area were taxed as
though it were in full use. No one could afford to own unused
land if such a tax system were adopted, and thus the only pos-
sessor of land would be the user. No landlord could arbitrar-
ily raise the price of land, as Butler does in "Under the Lion's
Paw," because there would be no landlords.

Garland occasionally introduced George's beliefs directly
into his stories, as when Grant McLane in "Up the Coulé"
comments on the evils of land speculation. But for the most
part his economic theories inform the stories of *Main-Travelled
Roads* in two oblique but important ways. One is in his dramatization of the mortgage as the major source of fear in
western life. The prospect of foreclosure haunts almost all the
farmers of *Main-Travelled Roads*. The other is in the tone of in-
dignation which characterizes his depiction of the hardships
and bleakness of western life, a tone which emerges out of his
conviction that these conditions are the product of an unjust
land system rather than attributable either to the farmers or
to the land. In his review of *Main-Travelled Roads* in 1891,
Howells noted that Garland's style exhibited "a certain

harshness and bluntness." This quality was already present in Garland's journal entries of 1887. For as he made his way west, Garland was responding with undisguised anger as he viewed the fear-ridden, labor-racked, unfulfilled lives of these his own people.

In his autobiography *A Son of the Middle Border* Garland implied that he returned from his 1887 trip white with anger and immediately dashed off the stories of *Main-Travelled Roads*. His belief that he wrote the stories at this time stems from his mistaken recollection that he made a second summer journey to the West in 1889. Since he had published two of the stories of *Main-Travelled Roads* by September, 1889, he later assumed that these and the other stories of the collection must be the product of his trip of 1887. In fact, Garland returned to Boston in the fall of 1887 and during the next nine months completed an unpublished Dakota novel and wrote the autobiographical sketches of "Boy Life on the Prairie" and a few short stories, none of which are in *Main-Travelled Roads*. In the summer of 1888 (not 1889, which he spent in the East), he again visited the West, and it was this trip which was the major stimulus for the composition of the stories of *Main-Travelled Roads*. Garland had begun to participate actively in the Henry George movement in November, 1887. During his journey to the West the following summer, he encountered at first hand the hard times which the droughts of 1887 and 1888 had brought to the Mississippi Valley. In addition, Garland's mother suffered a paralytic stroke during his visit to the family farm on the parched Dakota prairie. Thus, he returned to Boston in the fall of 1888 with an intense awareness of worsening social and family conditions and a fully aroused social conscience. His experiments in autobiography and fiction during 1887–88 had given him greater control of his craft than he possessed in late 1887, and his sense of purpose, of righteous anger, was now at fever pitch. From the fall of 1888 to early 1890 Garland wrote the best of his short fiction, including not only the stories of *Main-Travelled Roads* but also a number of excellent stories collected in *Prairie Folks* (1893).

Although there has been some confusion about when the stories of *Main-Travelled Roads* were written, there is little doubt about the specific source of almost every story. "A Branch-Road" was inspired by Garland's encountering at Osage a worn and haggard farm wife who had been a classmate at the Cedar Valley Seminary. "Up the Coulé" and "The Return of a Private" are autobiographical stories. The first depicts Garland as Howard McLane, a successful actor who is visiting his family in the West; the second is an account of the return of Garland's father from the Civil War, an account so close to the fact that Garland later used most of it unchanged in *A Son of the Middle Border*. "Among the Corn-Rows" was drawn in part from Garland's Dakota novel, and "Mrs. Ripley's Trip" was based on an anecdote told by his mother. Only "Under the Lion's Paw" lacks a specific source, a circumstance which suggests the pervasiveness of its situation in western life.

Garland had great difficulty in publishing his work. One of his most bitter stories, "John Boyle's Conclusion," which deals with the suicide of a Dakota farmer, was rejected by several magazines before it was accepted by a minor radical journal. The journal suspended several years later without having published the story.[5] Other such stories had parallel fates—rejection by the major journals (the *Atlantic Monthly*, *Harper's Monthly*, and the *Century*), acceptance by minor ones, or total rejection. *Harper's Weekly* published three of his stories, but all were relatively short for a Garland story and only

"Under the Lion's Paw" was openly radical. "Up the Coulé" and "A Branch-Road," two of Garland's longest and best stories of this period, found no outlet. It was with considerable joy, therefore, that Garland discovered B. O. Flower, editor of the *Arena*, a radical but widely read Boston monthly which had begun to appear in December, 1889. In the spring of 1890 Flower accepted Garland's "A Prairie Heroine," a story of the physical and spiritual dissolution of an overworked farm wife which had been rejected by several magazines. Flower welcomed its bitter tone, asked for more like it, and paid promptly and well. For more than two years a Garland article or story appeared in almost every issue of the *Arena*.

Early in 1891, Flower suggested that Garland collect some of his stories in a volume to be published by the Arena Publishing Company, a subsidiary enterprise of the *Arena*. Garland chose for the collection his two unpublished novelettes, which had apparently proven too long even for the *Arena*, and four of his published stories. *Main-Travelled Roads*, Garland's second book (his first was the radical play *Under the Wheel*, published in 1890), appeared simultaneously in hard and paper covers in early June, 1891. Garland's Boston friends, including Howells, gave the volume a good local press, but elsewhere it was less favorably received. The continuing agricultural depression had led to the formation of the Farmers' Alliance, a radical organization which elected several congressmen in 1890. By mid-1891 a fullscale farmers' party, the People's Party (or Populists), was in the planning stage for the election of 1892. Reviewers in the East therefore tended to associate Garland's intemperate tone with rebellious, ignorant farmers and to condemn both the tone and the farmers. Western reviewers, however, attacked the accuracy rather than the tone of Garland's portrayal of farm life. The

West, as they saw it, needed affirmation rather than negative and destructive criticism. As Garland later recalled,

I had a foolish notion that the literary folk of the west would take a local pride in the color of my work, and to find myself execrated by nearly every critic as "a bird willing to foul his own nest" was an amazement. Editorials and criticisms poured into the office, all written to prove that my pictures of the middle border were utterly false.

Statistics were employed to show that pianos and Brussels carpets adorned almost every Iowa farmhouse. Tilling the prairie soil was declared to be "the noblest vocation in the world, not in the least like the pictures this eastern author has drawn of it."[6]

The later history of *Main-Travelled Roads* is in part a history of Garland's literary career. During the early 1890s Garland led a divided life. He lectured on George's theories; he wrote radical stories, novels, and articles for the *Arena* and similar journals; and in 1892, he campaigned in Iowa for Populist candidates. But Garland was also anxious to achieve recognition and success as an "artist," to have his stories accepted and praised by such figures as Richard Watson Gilder, the poet-editor of the prestigious *Century*. By the mid-1890s Garland's career had moved firmly in this second direction. His radical fiction had been poorly received, and his most ambitious novel, *Rose of Dutcher's Coolly* (1895), had been viciously attacked for its sexual themes. Moreover, he had lost much of the personal fervor of his radicalism. In 1893 he "rescued" his parents from their Dakota farm and resettled them, in retirement, at West Salem. And in 1896 the Populist Party, Garland's major hope for the achievement of reform in the West, was absorbed into the Democratic Party, and both groups were defeated by McKinley Republicanism. Early in 1896 Garland undertook to write a biography of Ulysses S.

Grant, a project which occupied him for several years. When he returned to fiction in 1898 it was as the author of popular Rocky Mountain romances.

Throughout his radical years of the late 1880s and early 1890s Garland had written a kind of story which critical opinion, as reflected in the *Century* and its editor, held to be more "artistic" than the stories of *Main-Travelled Roads*. Known even in its own time as local color, this kind of story was usually set in far-off, quaint corners of America. Its tone was either light or nostalgic, and it made an effort to inform the reader about customs long-gone or unknown. Garland had written of the middle border in a nostalgic, informative vein from the very beginning of his career, as in his "Boy Life on the Prairie" sketches of 1888. In these and similar works, Garland permitted time to dull the sharp edge of experience, and his theme was that of the unusual customs and events of western life of the past. This theme appears only occasionally in the stories of the first edition of *Main-Travelled Roads*. Unfortunately, Garland in his later career chose to destroy the integrity of that edition by including stories written concurrently with those of the first edition but reflecting primarily a nostalgic attitude toward the West. He added three such stories in 1899, two in 1920, and a last in 1930. The impact of *Main-Travelled Roads* as a coherent and unified vision of western life was therefore weakened in these editions, and many readers who have encountered the book only in its later forms have been unable to appreciate either the historical significance or the permanent value of the 1891 collection.

All the stories of the 1891 *Main-Travelled Roads* have major flaws as stories, yet the book as a whole is powerful and evocative and has an aesthetic effect far superior to that of any one story. Garland's weaknesses as a writer of fiction, to discuss them first, are readily apparent. Throughout his career he had great difficulty with plot, and even his best stories contain inept narrative devices. For example, several of the stories of *Main-Travelled Roads* are marred by melodramatic and sentimental touches. The endings of "Under the Lion's Paw" and "A Branch-Road" resemble Victorian melodrama. In both stories the action is frozen at the close in a scene of heightened (and overwritten) moral crisis—Will demanding a decision from Agnes, Haskins threatening Butler. In both scenes a child suddenly appears either to add a touch of sentiment or to resolve the tension. Garland's difficulties with the mechanics of plot are particularly evident in his longer fiction. He often relies, in such works, on fortuitous events as a fictional crutch. Will's carriage accident in "A Branch-Road" plays this role, as does the lost letter in "Up the Coulé." Garland was on treacherous ground in the plotting of any long work of fiction and at the close of any short work—two occasions when narrative ability is put to its severest test.

Yet the book as a whole is artful and moving. One way in which Garland achieves these effects is by his road metaphor. The metaphor is introduced in the title, pursued in the dedication and preface, and maintained in the epigraphs to each story. The road is of course a traditional image of man's journey through life, but it was a particularly apt image for the West of Garland's time. The West in the late nineteenth century was indeed a main-travelled road, a place of constant coming and going, of settling and resettling, of departure and return. Both Garland and his family had experienced the West primarily as movement. The restlessness of Garland's father, the desire of his mother to put down roots, and Garland's own departures and returns had been the principal sources of tension in the family. It is not surprising, therefore, that Garland not only used the road image as an overt linking device in the collection as a whole but also structured each story around a physical move from one place to another. And it is of major significance that this move in every story is a return. The most obvious and, for Garland, most poignant kind of return is that of the successful figure to the people of his former world whom he had left behind to decay under the conditions of western life. "A Branch-Road" and "Up the Coulé" contain a return of this nature. But the motif also appears in the form of the return of the weary traveller from the great adventure of his life in order to take up again the burdens and hardships of daily existence, as in "The Return of a Private" and "Mrs. Ripley's Trip." Finally, in "Among the Corn-Rows" and "Under the Lion's Paw," characters who have ventured farther west return to older settlements of the middle border because of a flaw or inadequacy in their new world which they hope to correct in the old. The road image is thus the thematic and structural center of the book, for in every story the "end of the journey," the return, is to the unending toil of western life. Even Julia Peterson, who is escaping from the heavy field work of her father's Wisconsin farm in "Among the Corn-Rows" (the most buoyant story in the collection), will find that the labor of a Dakota kitchen and farmyard awaits her.

The return theme requires more detailed discussion in "A Branch-Road" and "Up the Coulé." The two stories dramatize Garland's sense of guilt toward his family and his fear that he will be unable to compensate them for his "desertion." In both stories the returning figure attempts to make amends for his negligence, but he can offer only pity and material comfort. In each instance farm life has taken its toll and crushed or permanently embittered the spirits of those left behind. Within this autobiographical theme the two stories contain another, less apparent, autobiographical element which has special significance for Garland's later career. Will Hannan and Howard McLane have attended a seminary; Will is studying to be a lawyer, and Howard has graduated and has been successful in the East. Each character responds to the conditions of western life in a manner appropriate to his superior training and experience. Will is disturbed by the crude behavior of the farm hands at the threshing, and Howard is affronted by the ugliness of farm life. Both characters are socially and aesthetically superior to western life,[7] and Garland associates their superiority with a failure or limitation of sympathy. Will fails to consider the feelings of Agnes in the first part of "A Branch-Road," and Howard has failed to consider that his family might be in need. Garland's joining of superiority and selfishness into a single theme has a twofold meaning for his work and career. The theme represents the particular configuration which he gave to his powerful sense of guilt in his early work. But the theme also anticipates his gradual estrangement from his area. For once Garland rescued his family, as he did in 1893, his sense of social and aesthetic superiority to the middle border became his dominant response and thus precluded his permanent involvement in its life either as person or as artist. During his later career the middle border inspired in him a genteel revulsion as he compared its ugliness and its failures in taste and decorum with the scenic grandeur of the Far West or the cultural richness of New York and London. In "A Branch-Road" and "Up the Coulé" revulsion is a functional and moving theme because it is inseparable from the pain and guilt of unfulfilled responsibility. Revulsion alone, however, was to lead Garland to flee the West as subject matter and as theme. And he was never to find another area of experience which engaged him as deeply as did the middle border in the late 1880s and early 1890s.

The stories of *Main-Travelled Roads* have another unifying element besides that of the road as theme and form. Although Garland had little talent for plot, he had a superb pictorial sense. *Main-Travelled Roads* can be described as a collection of landscapes and genre scenes. One such group of pictorial images juxtaposes the beauty of nature (a spring morning, a summer day, a sunset) and the ugliness and toil of farm activities. Another focuses on a man and a woman. The man is plowing in the mud on a cold autumn day. Every muscle of his body is straining and he is exhausted in body and spirit. The woman is at work in a dirty, cramped, hot kitchen. She is poorly dressed and goes about her tasks sullenly. The image of the man behind the plow was particularly moving to Garland (he had himself been that man, or youth), and he not only repeated it several times but also had Howard McLane imagine it as a landscape painting "by a master greater than Millet, a melancholy subject, treated with pitiless fidelity":

A farm in the valley! Over the mountains swept jagged, gray, angry, sprawling clouds, sending a freezing, thin drizzle of rain, as they passed, upon a man following a plough. The horses had a sullen and weary look, and their manes and tails streamed sidewise in the blast. The ploughman clad in a ragged gray coat, with uncouth, muddy boots upon his feet, walked with his head inclined toward the sleet, to shield his face from the cold and sting of it. The soil rolled away, black and sticky and with a dull sheen upon it.(96–97)

A final group of pictorial images is that of genre scenes—the threshing, the party at the McLanes, the Sunday dinner at Widow Gray's. Since the occasion is a holiday or an exciting group activity, the scene usually has a cheerful cast, though the reality or memory of intense labor is always present. These recurrent landscape and genre portraits (nature and farm, farmer and farm wife, and social gatherings) "illustrate" the road motif in the collection—the road of western life that is "hot and dusty in summer, and desolate and drear with mud in fall and spring," though it "does sometimes cross a rich meadow where the songs of the larks and bobolinks and blackbirds are tangled" (5).

Main-Travelled Roads is an important historical document. It portrays more vividly than any work of its time the physical and social conditions which led to the Populist revolt. But the book is also art. Despite his weaknesses as a writer of fiction, Garland found in the images of his youth a means of successfully imposing theme and form upon his experiences and his feelings. Road and picture, rather than plot, constitute the permanently moving in the stories of the collection. Since Garland was seldom to write as well again, his later work has adversely influenced the reputation of his early fiction. But in the 1891 *Main-Travelled Roads* Garland did write well, and the book deserves more credit for its intrinsic merits than it has usually received.

13

Stephen Crane's
Maggie and American Naturalism

S TEPHEN CRANE'S *MAGGIE: A Girl of the Streets* has
often served as an example of naturalistic fiction in
America. Crane's novel about a young girl's fall and death in
the New York slums has many of the distinctive elements of
naturalistic fiction, particularly a slum setting and the theme
of the overpowering effect of environment. Crane himself appeared to supply a naturalistic gloss to the novel when he
wrote to friends that *Maggie* was about the effect of environment on human lives. Yet the novel has characteristics which
clash with its neat categorization as naturalistic fiction. For
one thing, Crane's intense verbal irony is seldom found in
naturalistic fiction; for another, Maggie herself, though she
becomes a prostitute, is strangely untouched by her physical
environment. She functions as an almost expressionistic symbol of inner purity uncorrupted by external foulness. There is
nothing, of course, to prevent a naturalist from depending on
irony and expressionistic symbolism, just as there is nothing
to prevent him from introducing a deterministic theme into a
Jamesian setting. But in practice the naturalist is usually di-

rect. He is concerned with revealing the blunt edge of the powerful forces which condition our lives, and his fictional technique is usually correspondingly blunt and massive. When Zola in *L'Assommoir* and *Nana* wished to show the fall into prostitution of a child of the slums, his theme emerged clearly and ponderously from his full description of the inner as well as outer corruption of Nana and from his "realistic" symbolism. Crane's method, on the other hand, is that of obliqueness and indirection. Irony and expressionistic symbolism ask the reader to look beyond literal meaning, to seek beyond the immediately discernible for the underlying reality. Both are striking techniques which by their compelling tone and their distortion of the expected attempt to shock us into recognition that a conventional belief or an obvious "truth" may be false and harmful. Perhaps, then, *Maggie* can best be discussed by assuming from the first that Crane's fictional techniques imply that the theme of the novel is somewhat more complex than the truism that young girls in the slums are more apt to go bad than young girls elsewhere.[1]

The opening sentence of *Maggie* is: "A very little boy stood upon a heap of gravel for the honor of Rum Alley."[2] The sentence introduces both Crane's theme and his ironic technique. By juxtaposing the value of honor and the reality of a very little boy, a heap of gravel, and Rum Alley, Crane suggests that the idea of honor is inappropriate to the reality, that it serves to disguise from the participants in the fight that they are engaged in a vicious and petty scuffle. Crane's irony emerges out of the difference between a value which one imposes on experience and the nature of experience itself. His ironic method is to project into the scene the values of its participants in order to underline the difference between their values and reality. So the scene has a basic chivalric cast. The very little boy is a knight fighting on his citadel of gravel for the honor of his chivalrous pledge to Rum Alley. Crane's opening sentence sets the theme for *Maggie* because the novel is essentially about man's use of conventional but inapplicable abstract values (such as justice, honor, duty, love, and respectability) as weapons or disguises. The novel is not so much about the slums as a physical reality as about what people believe in the slums and how their beliefs are both false to their experience and yet function as operative forces in their lives.

Let me explore this idea by examining first the lives of the novel's principal characters and then the moral values which control their thinking about their lives. Crane uses two basic images to depict the Bowery. It is a battlefield and it is a prison. These images appear clearly in the novel's first three chapters, which describe an evening and night in the life of the Johnson family during Maggie's childhood. The life of the family is that of fierce battle with those around them and among themselves. The novel opens with Jimmie fighting the children of Devil's Row. He then fights one of his own gang. His father separates them with a blow. Maggie mistreats the babe Tommie; Jimmie strikes Maggie; Mrs. Johnson beats Jimmie for fighting. Mr. and Mrs. Johnson quarrel. Mrs. Johnson beats Maggie for breaking a plate; Mr. Johnson strikes Jimmie with an empty beer pail. Mr. Johnson comes home drunk and he and Mrs. Johnson fight—all this in three rather short chapters. Crane's fundamental point in these chapters is that the home is not a sanctuary from the struggle and turmoil of the world but is rather where warfare is even more intense and where the animal qualities encouraged by a life of battle—strength, fear, and cunning—predominate. The slum and the home are not only battlefields, however, but are also enclosed arenas. Maggie's tenement is in a "dark region," and her apartment, "up dark stairways and along cold, gloomy halls" (12, 15), is like a cave. Crane's description of the Johnson children eating combines both the warfare and cave images into one central metaphor of primitive competition for food: "The babe sat with his feet dangling high from a precarious infant chair and gorged his small stomach. Jimmie forced, with feverish rapidity, the grease-enveloped pieces between his wounded lips. Maggie, with side glances of fear of interruption, ate like a small pursued tigress" (19–20). By means of this double pattern of imagery, Crane suggests that the Johnsons' world is one of fear, fury, and darkness, that it is a world in which no moral laws are applicable, since the Johnsons' fundamental guide to conduct is an instinctive amorality, a need to feed and to protect themselves.

Once introduced, this image of the Bowery as an amoral, animal world is maintained throughout *Maggie*. Mr. Johnson dies, Jimmie assumes his position, and the Johnsons' family warfare continues as before. Maggie and Jimmie go to work, and each finds that struggle and enclosure mark his adult world. Jimmie becomes a belligerent truck driver, imprisoned by his ignorance and his distrust. He respects only strength in the form of the red fire engine which has the power to crush his wagon. Maggie works in a prisonlike sweat shop where she is chided into resentment by her grasping employer. Theirs are lives of animal struggle and of spiritual bleakness in which they only faintly realize their own deprivation. Maggie sits with the other girls in her factory workroom in a vague state of "yellow discontent," and Jimmie, the brawling teamster, "nevertheless . . . , on a certain starlit evening, said wonderingly and quite reverently: 'Deh moon looks like hell, don't it?' " (40).

The moral values held by the Johnsons are drawn almost entirely from a middle-class ethic which stresses the home as the center of virtue, and respectability as the primary moral goal. It is a value system oriented toward approval by others, toward an audience. In the opening chapter of the novel, Jimmie hits Maggie as Mr. Johnson is taking them home. Mr. Johnson cries, " 'Leave yer sister alone *on the street*' " (14) (my italics). The Johnsons' moral vision is dominated by moral roles which they believe are expected of them. These roles bring social approbation, and they are also satisfying because the playing of them before an audience encourages a gratifying emotionalism or self-justification. The reaction to Maggie's fall is basically of this nature. She is cast out by her mother and brother for desecrating the Home, and her se-ducer, Pete, rejects her plea for aid because she threatens the respectability of the rough and tumble bar in which he works. The moral poses adopted by the Johnsons and by Pete have no relation to reality, however, since the home and the bar are parallel settings of warfare rather than of virtue.

The key to the morality of the Bowery is therefore its self-deceiving theatricality. Those expressing moral sentiments do so as though playing a role before a real or implied audi-ence. Crane makes the dramatic nature of Bowery morality explicit in scenes set in dance halls and theatres. In a dance hall, an audience of Maggies, Jimmies, and Petes listens en-raptured to a song "whose lines told of a mother's love and a sweetheart who waited and a young man who was lost at sea under the most harrowing circumstances" (61–62). Later, Maggie and Pete see plays in which the

heroine was rescued from the palatial home of her guardian, who is cruelly after her bonds, by the hero with the beautiful sentiments. . . . Maggie lost herself in sympathy with the wanderers swooning in snow storms beneath happy-hued church windows. And a choir within singing "Joy to the World." To Maggie and the rest of the audience this was transcendental realism. Joy always within, and they, like the actor, inevitably without. Viewing it, they hugged themselves in ecstatic pity of their imagined or real condition. (70)

The audience identifies itself with maligned and innocent virtue despite the inapplicability of these roles to their own lives. "Shady persons in the audience revolted from the pictured villainy of the drama. With untiring zeal they hissed vice and applauded virtue. Unmistakably bad men evinced an apparently sincere admiration for virtue" (71).

This same ability to project oneself into a virtuous role is present in most of the novel's characters. Each crisis in the Johnson family is viewed by neighbors who comprise an audience which encourages the Johnsons to adopt moral poses. In the scene in which Maggie is cast out, both Jimmie and Mrs. Johnson are aware of their need to play the roles of outraged virtue in response to the expectations of their audience. Mrs. Johnson addresses the nieghbors "like a glib showman," and with a "dramatic finger" points out to them her errant daughter (132–33). The novel's final scene is a parody of Bowery melodrama. Mrs. Johnson mourns over the dead Maggie's baby shoes while the neighbors cry in sympathy and the "woman in black" urges her to forgive Maggie. In the midst of her exhortations, "The woman in black raised her face and paused. The inevitable sunlight came streaming in at the windows" (161). Crane in this scene connects the sentimental morality of melodrama and the sactimoniousness of Bowery religion. Both the theatre and the mission purvey moral attitudes which have no relation to life but which rather satisfy emotional needs or social approval. The heroes and heroines of melodrama cannot be confronted with reality, but the church is occasionally challenged. When it is, as when the mission preacher is asked why he never says "we" instead of "you," or when Maggie seeks aid from the stout clergyman, its reaction is either nonidentification with reality (" 'What?' " asks the preacher) or withdrawal from it (the clergyman sidesteps Maggie). It is as though the church, too, were a sentimental theatre which encouraged moral poses but which ignored the essential nature of itself and its audience.

Both of these central characteristics of the Bowery—its core of animality and its shell of moral poses—come together strikingly in Mrs. Johnson. There is a bitter Swiftian irony in Crane's portrait of her. Her drunken rages symbolize the animal fury of a slum home, and her quickness to judge, condemn, and cast out Maggie symbolizes the self-righteousness of Bowery morality. In a sense she symbolizes the entire Bowery world, both its primitive amorality and its sentimental morality. It is appropriate, then, that it is she who literally drives Maggie into prostitution and eventual death. Secure in her moral role, she refuses to allow Maggie to return home after her seduction by Pete, driving her into remaining with Pete and then into prostitution. Maggie is thus destroyed not so much by the physical reality of slum life as by a middle-class morality imposed on the slums by the missions and the melodrama, a morality which allows its users both to judge and to divorce themselves from responsibility from those they judge.

Crane's characterization of Maggie can now be examined. His description of her as having "blossomed in a mud puddle" with "none of the dirt of Rum Alley . . . in her veins" (41) is not "realistic," since it is difficult to accept that the slums would have no effect on her character. Zola's portrait of Nana dying of a disfiguring disease which symbolizes her spiritual as well as physical corruption is more convincing. Crane's desire, however, was to stress that the vicious deterministic force in the slums was its morality, not its poor housing or inadequate diet, and it is this emphasis which controls his characterization of Maggie. His point is that Maggie comes through the mud puddle of her physical environment untouched. It is only when her environment becomes a moral force that she is destroyed. Maggie as an expressionistic symbol of purity in a mud puddle is Crane's means of enforcing his large irony that purity is destroyed not by concrete evils but by the very moral codes established to safeguard it.

But Maggie is a more complex figure than the above analysis suggests. For though her world does not affect her moral nature, it does contribute to her downfall by blurring her vision. Her primary drive in life is to escape her mud puddle prison, and she is drawn to Pete because his apparent strength and elegance offer a means of overcoming the brutality and ugliness of her home and work. Her mistaken conception of Pete results from her enclosed world, a world which has given her romantic illusions just as it has supplied others with moral poses. Her mistake warrants compassion, however, rather than damnation and destruction. She is never really immoral. Throughout her fall, from her seduction by Pete to her plunge into the East River, Crane never dispels the impression that her purity and innocence remain. Her weakness is compounded out of the facts that her amoral environment has failed to arm her with moral strength (she "would have been more firmly good had she better known why" [115]), while at the same time it has blinded her with self-destructive romantic illusions ("she wondered if the culture and refinement she had seen imitated . . . by the heroine on the stage, could be acquired by a girl who lived in a tenement house and worked in a shirt factory" [72–73]).

There is considerable irony that in choosing Pete, Maggie flees into the same world she wished to escape. Like Mrs. Johnson, Pete desires to maintain the respectability of his "home," the bar in which he works. Like her, he theatrically purifies himself of guilt and responsibility for Maggie's fall as he drunkenly sobs " 'I'm good f'ler, girls' " (150) to an audi-

ence of prostitutes. And like Maggie herself, he is eventually
a victim of sexual warfare. He is used and discarded by the
"woman of brilliance and audacity" just as he had used and
discarded Maggie. In short, Maggie can escape the immediate prison of her home and factory, but she cannot escape being enclosed by the combination of amoral warfare (now sexual) and moral poses which is the pervasive force in her
world.

In his famous inscription to *Maggie*, Crane wrote that the
novel "tries to show that environment is a tremendous thing
in the world and frequently shapes lives regardless." But he
went on to write that "if one proves that theory one makes
room in Heaven for all sorts of souls (notably an occasional
street girl) who are not confidently expected to be there by
many excellent people."[3] The second part of the inscription
contains an attack on the "many excellent people" who, like
Maggie's mother, immediately equate a fallen girl with evil
and hell. Crane is here not so much expressing a belief in
heaven as using the idea of salvation and damnation as a rhetorical device to attack smug, self-righteous moralism. The
entire novel bears this critical intent. Crane's focus in *Maggie*
is less on the inherent evil of slum life than on the harm done
by a false moral environment imposed on that life. His irony
involving Mrs. Johnson, for example, centers on the religious and moral climate which has persuaded her to adopt the
moral poses of outraged Motherhood and despoiled Home.

Maggie is thus a novel primarily about the falsity and destructiveness of certain moral codes. To be sure, these codes
and their analogous romantic visions of experience are present in Maggie's environment, and are in part what Crane
means when he wrote that environment shapes lives regardless. But Crane's ironic technique suggests that his primary
goal was not to show the effects of environment but to distin-

guish between moral appearance and reality, to attack the sanctimonious self-deception and sentimental emotional gratification of moral poses. He was less concerned with dramatizing a deterministic philosophy than in assailing those who apply a middle class morality to victims of amoral, uncontrollable forces in man and society. *Maggie* is therefore very much like such early Dreiser novels as *Sister Carrie* and *Jennie Gerhardt*, though Dreiser depends less on verbal irony and more on an explicit documentation and discussion of the discrepancy between an event and man's moral evaluation of an event. *Maggie* is also like *The Red Badge of Courage*, for the later novel seeks to demonstrate the falsity of a moral or romantic vision of the amorality which is war.

Crane, then, is a naturalistic writer in the sense that he believes that environment molds lives. But he is much more than this, for his primary concern is not a dispassionate, pessimistic tracing of inevitable forces but a satiric assault on weaknesses in social morality. He seems to be saying that though we may not control our destinies, we can at least destroy those systems of value which uncritically assume we can. If we do this, a Maggie (or a Jennie Gerhardt) will at least be saved from condemnation and destruction by an unjust code.

Writers who seek greater justice, who demand that men evaluate their experience with greater clarity and honesty, are not men who despair at the nature of things. They are rather critical realists. Like William Dean Howells, Crane wishes us to understand the inadequacies of our lives so that we may improve them. Although Crane stresses weaknesses in our moral vision rather than particular social abuses, there is more continuity between Howells's critical realism and Crane's naturalism than one might suspect. This continuity is not that of subject matter or even of conception of man and society. It is rather that of a belief in the social function of the novel in delineating the evils of social life. If one sees such a writer as Crane in this light, the often crude and outdated determinism of early American naturalism lessens in importance. One begins to realize that American naturalism, like most vital literary movements, comprised a body of convention and assumption about the function and nature of literature which unprescriptively allowed the writer to use this shared belief as the basis for a personally expressive work of art. Crane's fiction is therefore permanently absorbing and historically significant not because he was a determinist or fatalist writing about the slums or about the chaos of war. His fiction still excites because his ironic technique successfully involves us in the difference between moral appearance and reality in society. His fiction is historically important because his expression of this theme within the conventions of naturalistic fiction reveals the relationship between critical realism and naturalism. But his fiction is perhaps even more significant historically because he revealed the possibility of a uniquely personal style and vision within naturalistic conventions. Our writers have responded to the critical spirit and the fictional sensationalism and freedom of naturalism without a sense of being burdened by doctrinaire precepts and forms. And it is no doubt this invigorating freedom within continuity which has been one of the principal reasons for the strength and influence of the naturalistic movement in America, from Crane and Dreiser to our own times.

14

Synthetic Criticism and Frank Norris's *The Octopus*

O NE OF THE most significant movements in the interpretation of American literature during the 1950s
and 1960s was the revitalization of the critical method pio-
neered by V. L. Parrington in the 1920s. Like Parrington,
such writers as Marius Bewley, Richard Chase, Leslie Fiedler,
and Leo Marx synthesized "main currents" in American literature and thought. Again like Parrington, they posited initially a universal dialectic in American experience which accounts for the distinctively American quality of these patterns
in our culture. In many ways this movement was estimable.
It illumined large areas of our national experience and expression. It also proved that a brilliant critic can forge intellectual history and myth criticism into an exciting and revealing tool of cultural research.

Yet despite my admiration for much synthetic criticism, I
am troubled by certain misgivings and reservations concerning its usefulness as a tool of literary criticism, and would like
to explain these doubts. My example of a work of synthetic
criticism is Leo Marx's "Two Kingdoms of Force,"[1] an arti-

cle which I will examine in relation to Frank Norris's *The Octopus*. I choose Mr. Marx as an example of a synthetic critic because I find him the most satisfying and the most suggestive of the group I have named, and am therefore moved to examine his critical method as representative of the group. I choose *The Octopus* as my example of a literary work not because I wish to explicate it (I have published explications elsewhere), and not because Mr. Marx's comments on it are more or less satisfying than those on other works. Rather, I know more about Norris's novel than any other work discussed by Mr. Marx, and can best demonstrate my general thesis by using it. In addition, I will introduce W. F. Taylor's *The Economic Novel in America* to help clarify the issues involved in my discussion.

Mr. Marx believes that a "common denominator" in much American literature is "the opposition between two cardinal images of value. One usually is an image of landscape, either wild or, if cultivated, rural; the other is an image of industrial technology." This opposition is not the result of a writer's direct reference to the historical fact of industrialism. Rather, the impact of industrialism has caused opposing "psychic states" to cluster around the opposing images of the landscape and the machine. These states are above all those suggesting love on the one hand and power on the other—that is, accommodation to the organic creativity of nature or dominion over nature. Though at first certain romantic writers (Hawthorne, Thoreau) consciously symbolized this opposition by means of images of nature and the machine, within a short time the dramatic clash between nature and machine became crystallized into a literary convention whose use suggests a writer's subconscious acceptance of the conflict rather than his explicit reference to it. Whether conscious or not, however, the polarity between the kingdom of love and the

kingdom of power—almost always represented by images of
nature and technology—is to Mr. Marx "a dominant, probably *the* dominant theme in our literature."

In a key passage, Mr. Marx explains that in *Huckleberry
Finn* the destruction of the raft by the steamboat reveals
Twain's participation in this theme despite Twain's avowed
faith in industrial progress and despite his lack of conscious
symbolism in the incident. "In the face of a discrepancy,"
Mr. Marx writes, "between what a writer tells us directly, in
his own words, so to speak, and what is implied by his work,
it is to his work that we owe the more serious attention. As between mere opinion and the indirection of art, we assume
that art springs from the more profound and inclusive experience."

Almost all the literary works and passages cited by Mr.
Marx to support his view are highly persuasive, including the
scene in *The Octopus* in which Presley experiences the massacre of a flock of sheep by a railroad engine. This incident, Mr.
Marx points out, destroys the idyllic calm of the scene as well
as Presley's sense of oneness with nature. Norris's presentation of the railroad and nature thus appears little different
from that of a Hawthorne or Thoreau. Mr. Marx concludes:
"Presley listens to the agonized cries of the wounded animals
and the blood seeping down into the cinders, *and thus the theme
of the novel is set.*"[2]

In his discussion of *The Octopus*, Mr. Marx has followed a
procedure common in synthetic criticism: the critic derives a
broad pattern from particular images, passages, and scenes
in a large number of works by many authors; he then implies
that this pattern is the key to the themes of individual works.
The opportunities for error and misdirection in this method
are familiar to readers of doctoral dissertations which survey
extensive material. In such works the student establishes a

tradition, "places" particular authors in this tradition, and finally deduces an interpretation and evaluation of individual works in terms of the author's tradition. On a more sophisticated level the same danger is inherent in works of synthetic criticism.

Let me begin to explain more concretely the source of my doubts about synthetic criticism by comparing Mr. Marx's interpretation of late nineteenth-century American fiction with that of W. F. Taylor, who has written one of the standard works on the subject. Mr. Taylor studies the economic fiction (in a broad sense) of most of the major figures of the age— Howells, Twain, Norris, and Garland—and of many minor writers as well. He believes that the novelists of this period

put on record—indeed, with virtual unanimity they put on *favorable* record—the coming of the Machine. Seldom if ever do they make the machine *per se* the object of critical attack. . . . In America, in the course of the conquest of the immense distances, the immense resources of a continent, the usefulness of the Machine was a thing difficult indeed to call in question; and, whether because of a tacit understanding of that difficulty, or because of some other causative factor, American novelists practically never did so. Instead, they mostly agreed with Mark Twain in welcoming the Machine, seeing in mechanical power, properly controlled, simply a means of realizing the old democratic dream of universal material well-being.

What our novelists put on *un*favorable record, what they subjected to telling exposure and criticism, was not the Machine itself but the misuse of the Machine by Society; not industrialism *per se*, but the workings of an industrial order administered by a *laissez-faire* capitalism.[3]

Mr. Taylor thus states a "pattern" antithetical to Mr. Marx's. If one reads *The Octopus* in terms of Mr. Taylor, its theme is the misuse of the machine by an uncontrolled monopoly rather than distrust and fear of the machine itself. But perhaps the antithesis between Mr. Marx and Mr. Taylor demonstrates not that one is right and the other wrong, but that *The Octopus* is a complex novel which is many things to many critics. Perhaps, too, this antithesis can be resolved by a reading of the novel which tries to come to grips with its own intrinsic pattern.[4]

Norris borrowed from Joseph LeConte, one of his teachers at the University of California, the idea that God is immanent in nature as a universal force or energy, and he used this idea as the core theme of *The Octopus*. As Presley views the harvested wheat fields toward the end of the novel, he "seemed for one instant to touch the explanation of existence." The explanation is that "FORCE only existed—FORCE that brought men into the world, FORCE that crowded them out of it to make way for the succeeding generation, FORCE that made the wheat grow, FORCE that garnered it from the soil to give place to the succeeding crop." This universal force inherent in the life processes of both human and nonhuman existence is finally characterized by Presley as "primordial energy flung out from the hand of the Lord God himself, immortal, calm, infinitely strong."[5] In *The Octopus* this energy is symbolized primarily by the wheat and by the processes of its growth and the "laws" of its production and distribution. Although these processes and laws are impersonal, they benefit the race as a whole. Individuals or groups determine their personal destinies by recognizing these processes—that is, by recognizing God in nature—and by tuning their lives in accord with them.

The moral center of the novel is thus nature, and evil is the failure to understand the processes of nature or the attempt to thwart them. Within this thematic core, the novel has a twofold structure. First, three overly intellectual and fundamentally selfish young men—Annixter, Vanamee, and Presley—come to accept the benevolence and the omnipotence of the natural cycle of birth, death, and rebirth. By this action, they rise above their personal sorrows and narrowness, and thereby achieve contentment and a resolution of their problem. Second, the ranchers and the railroad fail to realize the omnipotence and benevolence of the natural law of supply and demand which determines the production and the distribution of wheat. Both groups greedily exploit the demand for wheat, the first by speculative "bonanza" farming, the second by monopoly of transportation. Norris hammers at this similarity early in Book 2 in parallel images of the ranchers and railroad "sucking dry" the land. First, he describes a railroad map of California, on which the railroad's lines are drawn in red:

The map was white, and it seemed as if all the colour which should have gone to vivify the various counties, towns, and cities marked upon it had been absorbed by that huge, sprawling organism, with its ruddy arteries converging to a central point. It was as though the State had been sucked white and colourless, and against this pallid background the red arteries of the monster stood out, swollen with life-blood, reaching out to infinity, gorged to bursting; an excrescence, a gigantic parasite fattening upon the life-blood of an entire commonwealth. (II,5)

The greed of the railroad is matched by that of the ranchers, however, for

they had no love for their land. They were not attached to the soil. They worked their ranches as a quarter of a century before they had worked their mines. To husband the resources of their marvellous San Joaquin, they considered niggardly, petty, Hebraic. To get all there was out of the land, to squeeze it dry, to exhaust it, seemed their policy. When, at last, the land worn out, would refuse to yield, they would invest their money in something else; by then, they would all have made fortunes. They did not care. "After us the deluge." (II,14)

Both groups, moreover, engaged in corrupt acts in their struggle for possession of the profitable land and its crop. There is no doubt, of course, that Norris considered the railroad trust the more culpable of the two, and that he indirectly suggested means of alleviating its hold upon the community. But Norris's primary emphasis was that the benevolent cycle of growth and the fulfilment of demand by supply are completed regardless of whatever harm and destruction men bring down upon themselves by their attempts to hinder or to manipulate these natural processes for their own profit.[6]

The symbolic role of the railroad engine throughout *The Octopus* is conditioned by the theme of the novel. Individual engines, such as that which destroys the flock of sheep, do not symbolize the machine as a power antithetical to that of nature. Rather, they symbolize a particular railroad company whose monopolistic practices are antithetical to a particular natural law. Norris underlines this symbolism at the close of the passage which ends the description of the sheep massacre:

Then, faint and prolonged, across the levels of the ranch, he heard the engine whistling for Bonneville. Again and again, at rapid intervals in its flying course, it whistled for road crossings, for sharp curves, for trestles; ominous notes, hoarse, bellowing, ringing with the accents of menace and defiance; and abruptly Presley saw again, in his imagination, the galloping monster, the terror of steel and steam, with its single eye, Cyclopean, red, shooting from horizon to horizon; but saw it now as the symbol of a vast power, huge, terrible, flinging the echo of its thunder over all the reaches of the valley, leaving blood and destruction in its path; the leviathan, with tentacles of steel clutching into the soil, the soulless Force, the iron-hearted Power, the monster, the Colossus, the Octopus. (I,48)

The engine, then, is above all a symbol of the Octopus— that is, the Trust. The monopoly is the soulless Force whose practices, spreading death and destruction, are opposed to

the landscape ("tentacles of steel clutching into the soil").
Norris desires to engage our emotions to fear and hate trusts,
not industrialism or the machine. His theme in the novel is
not the conflict between technology and nature or between
the kingdom of power and the kingdom of love, as Mr. Marx
suggests it is in his discussion of the sheep massacre scene.
His theme is that "all things, surely, inevitably, resistlessly
work together for good" (II,361), that technology and the
landscape are allied rather than opposed in the forward
thrust toward human betterment. They are allied, that is, so
long as men use both landscape and machine (the means of
production and distribution of wheat) in accordance with
natural law.

Norris illustrates this possible alliance by means of Cedarquist, a San Francisco industrialist and shipbuilder. Early in
Book 2 Cedarquist outlines to Magnus Derrick a plan where-
by the producers and distributors of wheat can use the law of
supply and demand in a way which benefits both themselves
and mankind. He explains:

The great word of this nineteenth century has been Production.
The great word of the twentieth century will be . . . Markets. As a
market for our Production—or let me take a concrete example—as
a market for our *Wheat*, Europe is played out. Population in Europe
is not increasing fast enough to keep up with the rapidity of our production. In some cases, as in France, the population is stationary.
We, however, have gone on producing wheat at a tremendous rate.
The result is overproduction. We supply more than Europe can eat,
and down go the prices. The remedy is *not* in the curtailing of our
wheat areas, but in this, we *must have new markets, greater markets*. For
years we have been sending our wheat from East to West, from
California to Europe. But the time will come when we must send it
from West to East. . . . I mean, we must look to China. Rice in
China is losing its nutritive quality. The Asiatics, though, must be
fed; if not on rice, then on wheat. . . . What fatuous neglect of op-

portunity to continue to deluge Europe with our surplus food when the East trembles upon the verge of starvation! (II,21–22)

On the basis of this perception, Cedarquist begins to ship wheat to the East. In short, the "mechanical" distributor (a railroad or shipping company) can with profit to himself aid the fulfillment of a benevolent natural law rather than attempt to thwart the operation of the law for excessive personal gain.

Norris therefore does establish a kingdom of love, but he not unconventionally suggests that it is the kingdom of self-love, of greed—not of power—which opposes it. In other words, Norris's basic attitude corresponds less to the artist's sense that there is a contradiction between the worlds of nature and the machine than to the capacity of the popular mind to maintain without a sense of contradiction the opposing ideals of cultural primitivism and industrial progress. Norris holds in solution, without conflict, both the kingdom of love (accommodation to nature) and of power (dominion over nature), just as most eighteenth-century Englishmen (as Lois Whitney has pointed out)[7] called for both a return to the simple and a progress toward the complex, and just as the average American feels no discrepancy in taking a jet to "get away from it all" in the North Woods.

Now in this cursory summary of *The Octopus* I have not taken up what Mr. Marx considers "direct" testimony as evidence concerning Norris's attitude toward the machine. I have not, for example, discussed his California background, in which the importance of the railroad to the well-being of the state was universally affirmed but in which the Southern Pacific monopoly was often referred to as an Octopus. I have not traced those occasions in Norris's fiction and criticism when he deals honorifically with the industrialist and with machines, including railroad engines. I have not introduced the influence of Kipling, who combined in such works as *Captains Courageous* an admiration both for the "natural" life and for railroads and their machinery. Nor have I discussed Zola's influence on Norris's depiction of destructive railroad engines and on his practice of animalizing machines. I have not taken up any of these, though they have all helped me to understand Norris's treatment of the railroad in *The Octopus*.

But to return to one of Mr. Marx's most pertinent ideas (which he introduces in connection with Huck's raft and the steamboat), that though a fictional incident may not be literally symbolic of a nature-machine conflict, it may draw upon the conventional imagery and connotations of such a conflict. This observation is applicable to *The Octopus*. Though Norris does not distrust the machine, he does mistrust monopolies. He therefore uses the conventional imagery of the machine-nature "pattern" to add emotional intensity to his engine-Octopus-Trust symbolism. In short, the machine-nature antithesis serves Norris as a reservoir of affective imagery, though it does not necessarily function as a thematic key.

Norris's exploitation of the machine as a source of such imagery is also demonstrated by a passage in which nature itself is presented as a destructive machine. In this passage, Norris wished to depict how the omnipotent and impersonal power of nature appears to a timid, withdrawn, and frightened person, one whose timidity prevents her from sensing the fundamental benevolence of this power. To Mrs. Derrick, therefore, the railroad and nature are equally destructive because of their power. She first imagines the railroad (repeating Presley's imagery) as a "galloping terror of steam and steel, with its single eye, Cyclopean, red," etc. (I,173). Then follows her conception of nature:

She recognized the colossal indifference of nature, not hostile, even kindly and friendly, so long as the human ant-swarm was submissive, working with it, hurrying along at its side in the mysterious march of the centuries. Let, however, the insect rebel, strive to make head against the power of this nature, and at once it became relentless, a gigantic engine, a vast power, huge, terrible; a leviathan with a heart of steel, knowing no compunction, no forgiveness, no tolerance, crushing out the human atom with soundless calm, the agony of destruction sending never a jar, never the faintest tremor through all that prodigious mechanism of wheels and cogs. (I,174)

Thus, it is apparent that Norris draws upon machine imagery to provide emotional intensity to the description of any destructive force, including nature itself when it is so conceived. This reliance does indeed imply that despite his overt emphasis on the benevolent role of the machine, Norris unconsciously participates in the "main current" described by Mr. Marx. But I do not think that it is possible on the basis of this participation to say that *The Octopus* is "really about" the two kingdoms of force—that is, that its theme is set by its imagery of the destructive machine.

Rather, I think it more meaningful to say that Mr. Taylor has seen that Norris's theme involves an attack on the misuse of the machine, and that Mr. Marx has seen that Norris relies on a traditional romantic description of the machine. Both have described parts of Norris's theme and art in *The Octopus*; neither has seen the novel whole; and neither, indeed, have I in this brief paper.

How, then, to strive for this "wholeness"? I would suggest a critical eclecticism. To know something of Norris's biography, of the intellectual and literary influences upon him, and of his social milieu—to read *The Octopus* with a sense of its total impact and with a recognition that its parts (including imagery and symbolism) should be relevant to that impact—and to know something about such cultural traditions as the "two kingdoms of force"—this seems to me to be the best method for determining the meaning and significance of a complex work of art. The conflict between the two kingdoms of force may well be the dominant theme in American literature, and Norris does partake of that theme in *The Octopus*. But the theme of *The Octopus* is not "set" by scenes in which one element is the conventional imagery of the destructive machine.

15

Jack London:
The Problem of Form

MOST OF THE significant criticism of Jack London has been devoted to two interrelated issues: Is there a coherent center to London's ideas or are they indeed hopelessly confused and contradictory; and what are the sources of London's strength and appeal as a writer given the superficiality of much of his work? So, for example, critics have often grappled with the relationship between London's socialism and Nietzscheanism, and they have sought to explain how a writer who could achieve the seamless perfection of "To Build a Fire" could also produce an extraordinary amount of trash. Whatever the value of these efforts, almost all have been piecemeal in character. The critic tackles a particular narrow problem or a specific work and then extrapolates from it. At the considerable risk of moving to the other extreme of overschematization and overgeneralization, I would like to suggest a single dominant solution to the enigma which is Jack London. The notion which I propose to pursue is that London as a thinker and as an artist is essentially a writer of fables and parables.

To help clear the ground, I should note that I do not maintain that there is a clear distinction between the fable and the parable.[1] Both forms are didactic. They seek to establish the validity of a particular moral truth by offering a brief story in which plot, character, and setting are allegorical agents of a paraphrasable moral. But historically, because of the association of fable with Aesop and of parable with the Bible, each of the terms also has a more specialized coloration. By fable is usually meant a work in which beasts (and occasionally inanimate objects) both speak and represent human qualities, and by parable is meant a work in which the principal agents are human. Furthermore, the moral of a fable is apt to be far more worldly than that of a parable. Fables deal with how men act on earth, parables with how they should act to gain salvation.

Fables and parables are not fiction in our modern sense of the distinctive nature of fiction. They simplify experience into useable precept rather than render it as either complex or ambivalent. But in that simplification lies a potential for artistic strength if artistry in this instance can be said to be the restatement in pleasing form of what we as a race or society wish to hear about ourselves. The special appeal of the beast fable is that it substitutes wit for insight; it expresses not deep or fresh perception but rather a concise and clever recapitulation of what everybody knows. In the beast fable foxes are always shrewd, lions bold, hawks predatory, sheep silly, asses stupid, and so on. Setting is nonexistent or minimal and when present is a condition of the moral dilemma in which the beasts find themselves (a forest is danger, a barn safety). And action is limited to that which renders immediately and clearly the heart of the precept.

Much of the attraction of the fable lies not only in our pleasure in finding clearly recognizable human characteristics confirmed in animals but in the nature of the precepts which these characteristics advance. For the wisdom of the fable is the ancient wisdom of the world—that the shrewd and strong prevail unless blinded by pride, that greed is a great equalizer, and so on. The lesson of the fable is that the world is a place of seeking and grasping in which specific qualities of human nature always receive their just dessert. In the fable, vanity is always victimized by shrewdness, disappointment always seeks rationalization, and desire for gain guides all life.

Parable often moves beyond the way we are to the way we should be. While the precept of a fable is both concrete and expedient (be less vain and you shall prosper more), that of a parable tends toward moral abstractions (be charitable and you will be a better person). And since the ability to frame and respond to moral abstractions is a distinctively human attribute, the personae in a parable are almost always human.

By the late nineteenth century, whatever lines of demarcation that might have existed earlier between fable and parable had for the most part disappeared. In Kipling's *The Jungle Book*, for example, the worldliness of the beast fable and the more programmatic moralism of the parable join in clear allegories containing both animal and human characters. It was to this blending of the fable/parable form that London was powerfully drawn.

It seems strange today that the principal critical issue for many early readers of the most obviously fabulistic of London's fiction, his dog stories, was their problematical accuracy in depicting the conditions of natural life. After the great success of *The Call of the Wild* and *White Fang* (as well as the contemporary popularity of other nature fiction), Theodore Roosevelt, in a famous controversy of 1907, attacked London (among others) as a "nature faker." Referring to the fight between a lynx and a wolf in *White Fang*, Roosevelt commented, "Nobody who really knew anything about either a lynx or a wolf would write such nonsense." He then went on to reveal his misunderstanding of the form in which London was writing. "If the stories of these writers were written in the spirit that inspired Mowgli [the human figure in Kipling's *The Jungle Book*], . . . we should be content to read, enjoy, and accept them as fables. . . . But when such fables are written by a make-believe realist, the matter assumes an entirely different complexion."[2]

Of course, criticism of London has advanced far beyond Roosevelt's demand that animal fiction should announce itself clearly as either fabulistic or realistic. For example, in a striking reading of *The Call of the Wild* and *White Fang*, Earle Labor has suggested that the permanent appeal of these works is that they are beast fables whose endorsement of the myth of the hero and of the value of primordial strength rings true in our collective unconscious.[3] Labor's Jungian reading of these works is the most useful which has yet appeared, but I believe that a more immediate reason for the appeal and holding power of London's best work lies in their form.

London's work falls roughly into three groups related to his "natural" inclination to work in the fable/parable form. The first, which includes *The Call of the Wild* and *White Fang* as well as such stories as "To Build a Fire" and "The Chinago," reveals his ability to rely unconsciously yet with great success on the underlying characteristics of the fable/parable. The second, which includes *The Iron Heel* and such stories as "The Apostate" and "The Strength of the Strong," suggests that when London wrote consciously in the parable form—as he did in these works—he sacrificed power for ideological obviousness. And the third, which includes a large number of

London's novels and short stories, but most significantly *The Sea-Wolf*, indicates that London's efforts to write conventional fiction were usually handicapped by his inadequacies in this form, but that such works are occasionally rescued by their fabulistic element. Finally, I will also suggest that much that is distinctive and valuable in London's autobiographical writing—in *The Road, Martin Eden,* and *John Barleycorn*—can be viewed as an extension into this form of his penchant for the fable/parable.

The Call of the Wild and *White Fang* are companion allegories of the response of human nature to heredity and environment. Both Buck and White Fang begin their lives with a mixture of the primitive and the civilized in their condition. Buck is raised in the Southland (London's allegorical setting for civilization), but, like all dogs, has an atavistic strain of wolf in his make-up. White Fang, though largely wolf and though bred in the Far North, contains an element of the civilized through his part-dog mother. The novels demonstrate the effects of a change in environment on the two dogs. Buck, abducted into a Northland world of the ruthless struggle for existence, calls forth from his racial past the strength and cunning necessary to survive in this world, and eventually becomes the leader of a wolf-pack in a people-less wilderness. White Fang is drawn into civilization, first by Indians, then by miners, and finally, in the Southland, by upper middle class ranchers, and becomes doglike in his loyalty and love toward his master.

What appeals in the two works is not London's dramatization of a particular late nineteenth-century Darwinian formulation but rather his powerful use of the principal ethical thrust and formal characteristics of the fable, with an admixture as well of the parable. Characterization is at a minimum in the two works; dogs and men are types and the types themselves are moral in nature. In *Call*, Charles, Hal, and Mercedes (the three "tenderfoot" Klondikers who buy Buck) are Vanity and Ignorance, and John Thornton is Loyalty and Love. The dogs in the story are even more clearly moral types—Laziness, Envy, Fear, Honesty, and so on. In *White Fang*, Kiche is the Mother, Beauty Smith (who exhibits White Fang) is Evil, and Weedon Scott is Thornton's counterpart. Setting is allegorical in both works, with London exaggerating for symbolic clarity both the "softness" of the South and the competitive animality of the North. And action is symbolic within the clear lines of thematic movement of Buck's return to the primitive and White Fang's engagement by civilization. Perhaps most important of all, theme itself is essentially proverbial rather than ideological. It is not so much Darwin and Spencer who supply the thematic core of the two novels as Aesop and the Bible. For *Call of the Wild* proposes the wisdom of the beast fable that the strong, the shrewd, and the cunning shall prevail when, as is progressively true in this story, life is bestial. And *White Fang* endorses the Christian wisdom that all shall lie down together in peace when love predominates.

Both *Call* and *White Fang* contain—to a degree not usually sufficiently stressed—a strong element of the Christian parable within their beast fable emphasis on the competitive nature of experience. Buck's response to the kindness, justness, and warmth of Thornton is love; it is only with the death of Thornton that he becomes the Ghost Dog of the wilderness. And White Fang, when rescued from the brutality of Beauty Smith by Weedon Scott and when "educated" in affection by Scott, also responds with love. The moral allegory is clear in both works. Man hovers between the primitive and the civilized both in his make-up and in his world, and it is his capacity for love which often determines which direction he will take. Again, this theme is not so much specifically ideological as it is racial wisdom, with that wisdom embodied in a form which makes it pleasingly evident.

An obvious question, given the similarities in theme and form between the two works, is why *The Call of the Wild* is generally held to be superior to *White Fang*. An answer lies, I believe, in the greater conformity of *Call* to the beast fable form in two significant areas. First, *White Fang* makes greater pretentions to the range and fulness of a novel. Fabulistic brevity and conciseness, and thus symbolic sharpness, are sacrificed for lengthy development of each phase of White Fang's career. And since we can anticipate from the beginning the nature and direction of his evolution, the doldrums occasionally set in. But also, as Earle Labor has pointed out, we are inherently more interested in an account of a return to the primitive than one of an advance into civilization. Labor suggests, as I noted earlier, that this difference in attraction lies in the greater appeal which *Call* makes to our unconscious longing for primitive simplicity and freedom. But this greater holding power may derive as well—and more immediately— from the fuller endorsement in *Call* of the Aesopian wisdom that the strong prevail. There is not much love in Aesop, but there is much demonstration that it is better to be powerful in a world in which power controls destiny.

London's best known and most admired story, "To Build a Fire," is also a fable/parable in the sense that I have discussed *The Call of the Wild* and *White Fang*. The story reveals London's ability to use the conventions of the form not only in works centering on animals but also in those in which human characters predominate. As in *Call* and *White Fang*, London in "To Build a Fire" (as well as in such a firstrate story as "The Chinago") involves us in a fable/parable without his conscious awareness that he is exploiting an allegory to deliver a message.[4] In "To Build a Fire," the *chechaquo*, or "newcomer in the land," is Ignorance, and the setting in which he finds himself, the extraordinary frost of a Yukon cold snap, is Danger. From its opening words, the fable moves toward its resolution of these two permanent conditions of life. As in London's dog stories, the moral of "To Build a Fire" rests more on racial wisdom than Darwinian ideology, just as in "The Chinago"—a story in which a Chinese coolie in Tahiti is wrongly executed for a murder—the fabulistic moral that men will destroy rather than acknowledge and rectify a mistake is more powerfully felt than any social protest theme arising out of the exploitation of coolie labor in the South Seas. In "To Build a Fire," the success of the story, as in the successful fable, stems from our acceptance of its worldly wisdom while simultaneously admiring the formal devices used to communicate it—in this instance, the ironic disparity between our knowledge of Danger and the newcomer's Ignorance of it, and the brevity and clarity of the story's symbolic shape.

Like many artists, London not only unconsciously exploited his own best talent but also consciously overexploited it on the one hand and neglected it on the other. Overexploitation occurs in a number of stories in which London consciously used the fable/parable form. In these works, of which "The Apostate" and "The Strength of the Strong" are perhaps the best known examples, London the ideologue is too fully in control of the mechanism of the story; that is, London as parablist dominates London as fabulist. "The Apostate," for example, was subtitled "A Child Labor Parable" in its magazine appearance,[5] and that is what it is—no more and no less. The story tells us, in its account of a young man who has worked from childhood in various mills and factories, that the effort to turn children and men into machines will breed rebellion, that the human body and soul are incapable of being fully mechanized. The parable is effective in its own right, but its success is on a lower level than that of "The Chinago." In that story the moralism inherent in the fable/parable form is rendered wryly rather than "preachingly." In "The Chinago," an innocent is also destroyed by "the system"—the bureaucracy of a judicial process which grinds to its conclusion even though the wrong man is being guillotined. The "way of the world" fabulist irony of the story—that for most men it is more important to get the job done and to do it well (the executioners take pride in the guillotine they have constructed) than to achieve justice—saves the story from the sermonizing effect of "The Apostate." This is not to say that "The Chinago" and "To Build a Fire" are not moral works; if their moralism were not preeminent, they would not be fables/parables. Rather it is to say that their moralism is less instructive (correct this evil) than informative (this is the way the world is) and that their tone is less indignant and somber than wry and detached.

London prefaced "The Strength of the Strong" with a brief epigraph: "Parables don't lie, but liars will parable." He attributed this aphorism to "Lip-King," and thus paid mock homage to the principal writer of fables and parables of his day, Kipling. (Indeed, Kipling is also present in the story itself in the figure of the "Bug," a poet and parablist who endorses the imperialist, capitalistic ethic of the tribal leaders.) Like "The Apostate," "The Strength of the Strong" has its origin in London's socialist convictions. The narrator of the story is one of the few survivors of a prehistoric tribe which was destroyed by its own selfish bickering. His account of tribal history is thus a history of civilization in which the parable moral is that when group interest is sacrificed to self-interest, the group is doomed. Whereas "The Apostate" lacks vitality, "The Strength of the Strong" is enlivened by the satiric edge of London's translation of various moments in Western history into comically rendered incidents in the history of a specific tribe. Nevertheless, the central thrust of the story is still that of a political sermon, of London offering a conscious rebuttal to the "Bug's" view of man's social nature and destiny.

It is London's proselytizing for a cause which also vitiates his major exercise in the fully conscious parable, *The Iron Heel*. Although the novel is often described as an anti-Utopia, it can also be profitably considered a parable despite its length. As in all of London's intentional parables, the "lesson" of *The Iron Heel* is single-dimensional: the forces arrayed against the achievement of social justice in America are powerful and ruthless. The work has its moments, particularly the Battle of Chicago conclusion, but its overall failure illustrates the dangers inherent in extending ideological parable beyond the brief narrative. Parable teaches best by example, but the expansiveness of *The Iron Heel* permits London too much opportunity to teach by argument in Everhard's lengthy explanations of the rightness of his cause. "The Strength of the Strong" is by far the better artistic rendering of London's social ideas because it is by far the better parable.

But what of one of London's most widely read novels, *The Sea-Wolf*? This compelling but seriously flawed work assumes its basic nature from London's effort to combine characteristics of the fable/parable with those of the conventional novel. The strengths of *The Sea-Wolf* (and a number of similar works in London's canon) are those of the fable/parable, the weaknesses those of the novel.

The Sea-Wolf contains a buried fable/parable which is the principal source of its fictional energy—that of the over-reacher. Wolf Larsen is less a character than a type. He is the man-as-wolf who not only acts and thinks wolfishly in his single-minded gratification of self but has the mental equipment to attempt to justify his nature. But though we may agree that there are many instances of wolflike behavior and values in life, we also agree that we are not a civilization of wolves, and we are thus more gratified than surprised when a parable element of moral retribution enters the fable of a wolf among us. He who lives by the code of animal strength will die by it, as Larsen indeed does when his vigor and shrewdness are diminished by a brain tumor. We find in the Wolf Larsen portion of *The Sea-Wolf* many of the characteristics which make *The Call of the Wild* so powerful a work: distinct moral types, symbolic setting (the ship and the sea in *The Sea-Wolf*), an allegorical narrative, and the whole mix pushing toward a fable/parable combination of worldly wisdom (the strong rule) and parable moralism (but not forever).

To this fable/parable core, London added some of the conventional ingredients of the novel in the characters and experiences of Humphrey Van Weyden and Maud Brewster. Unlike Larsen, who is unchanging in his beliefs and values, they are intended to be developing characters who undergo a significant transformation through experience. Whatever their origin in the conventions of popular initiation fiction of London's day, they are taken seriously by him as "realistic" fictional characters—that is, figures whose natures and motives are probable and believable. But London's effort to shape figures of this kind fails completely, for in Hump and Maud he has in fact created standard fictional types (effete and over-refined intellectuals) who undergo standard fictional transformations (they come to an understanding and use of strength in human affairs) and who thereby receive their just reward (survival and love). In short, whereas Wolf Larsen is acceptable and powerful because he is created and functions as a fabulistic type, Hump and Maud fail because London's inadequacies as a writer of fiction lead him to formulaic constructs, including type characters. The difference between Larsen on the one hand and Hump and Maud on the other, it should be clear, does not lie in the inherent greater appeal of one kind of figure over another. Characters undergoing initiatory experiences have been one of the great staples of major world literature, while the tyrannical sea captain has been a staple of superficial romance. The difference rather lies in London's ability to depict Wolf Larsen within the conventions of the fable/parable and his inability to deal with Hump and Maud within the conventions of the novel.

Much of London's best writing is autobiographical, whether in the form of autobiography with a considerable fictional element (as in *The Road* and *John Barleycorn*) or in the form of fiction which is closely autobiographical (as in *Martin Eden*). It is true that in these works the brevity of the fable/parable is sacrificed to the fulness of detail characteristic of modern autobiography. But in all other significant ways London adapts the conventions of the fable/parable to the needs of autobiographical expression and thereby achieves some striking successes. In each of his best autobiographies, London chooses a specific area of his life for representation, and in each the material of the experience is molded into a symbolic form which expresses a truth characteristic of the worldly wisdom of the fable. So in *The Road*, London's months as a hobo dramatize the process by which the concrete experience of injustice will stimulate a rebellion against it, in *John Barleycorn* his obsession with alcohol documents the limitations of human control of desire, and in *Martin Eden* his efforts to become a writer reveal that success, once gained, is not as sweet as it seemed.

Martin Eden suggests how London adapts one of the principal impulses of autobiography—to give meaning to one's life by the selective use of the material of one's life—to create a moral allegory closely related to the form of the fable/parable. In London's account of his attempt to become a successful writer, experience is good if it contributes to this goal, evil if it hinders. The work contains little complexity of characterization, even in such fully drawn figures as Ruth Morse and Russ Brissenden, and there is no plot—only obstacles, hazards, and momentary resting places in Martin's slow rise to knowledge and competency. Ruth is Martin's False Guide in this climb; he initially mistakes her for Truth because of her seeming spirituality, but he eventually realizes her weak conventionality. Brissenden is Truth—the truth that art must be rebellious—and also Martin's Fate. Brissenden's early alcoholic death and his difficulty in gaining acceptance dramatize the condition and destiny of the artist in America. Other figures are even more programmatic. Martin's sister and brother-in-law, for example, represent respectively family loyalty and grubbing materialism, while Ruth's family embodies upper class philistine smugness. Even ideas play a symbolic role in London's fable of the artist in America, since Martin's infatuation with the thought of Herbert Spencer signifies his need to find intellectual confirmation of his sense of himself as an independent being in a conforming world. Yet despite the blatancy of the allegorical mode in *Martin Eden*, the work lives because blatancy in this instance is functional within the fable/parable form of the work. Much of that which absorbs us in *Martin Eden* is attributable to its character as a fable of the American artist at odds with his world, temporarily victoriously over it, and finally defeated by it.

As in the best of his dog stories, London in *Martin Eden* (as well as in *The Road* and *John Barleycorn*) writes powerfully in the fable/parable form both because he is writing instinctively and unconsciously within the conventions of this form and because he ignores most of the conventions of the ostensible form he is writing in while drawing profitably upon others. London's strength as a writer was not so much to tell a story as to tell a story in order to demonstrate the truth of a specific moral which revealed the way of the world but which also often instructed in the way of the heart. (In *Martin Eden*, the friendship of Martin and Brissenden plays this second role.) The writer of fables and parables may not be either original or profound, but as the history of world literature demonstrates, and as London's reputation further illustrates, at his best he can engage us fully and permanently.

16

Theodore Dreiser's "Nigger Jeff": The Development of an Aesthetic

THANKS TO THE work of Robert H. Elias and W. A. Swanberg, we are beginning to have an adequate sense of Dreiser's life. But many aspects of Dreiser the artist remain relatively obscure or unexplored—in particular his aesthetic beliefs and fictional techniques at various stages of his career. An excellent opportunity to study Dreiser's developing aesthetic lies in the existence of several versions of his short story "Nigger Jeff." The extant versions of this story reveal with considerable clarity and force Dreiser's changing beliefs concerning the nature of fiction.

Dreiser's first attempt to write a story about the lynching of a Missouri Negro is preserved in an unpublished University of Virginia manuscript called "A Victim of Justice."[1] Although "A Victim of Justice" is clearly a work of the 1890s, it is difficult to date its composition precisely. The narrator of the story begins by noting that he has recently spent "a day in one of Missouri's pleasant villages." While visiting a Potter's Field, he recalls a rural Missouri lynching that he had witnessed "several years since." This opening situation is the product of a number of events of the mid-1890s. Dreiser was a reporter on the *St. Louis Republic* in the winter of 1893–94, and it was during this period that he observed the lynching on which the story is based.[2] In addition, on July 23, 1894, Dreiser wrote for the *Pittsburgh Dispatch* an article entitled "With the Nameless Dead" in which he described an Allegheny County Potter's Field. A few weeks later he visited his fiancee, Sallie White, who lived in a small town near St. Louis.[3] Dreiser's only attempts at fiction before the summer of 1899 occurred in the winter and spring of 1895 when he wrote several stories after leaving the *New York World* and before becoming editor of *Ev'ry Month*.[4] In view of these facts, it is possible to speculate that Dreiser wrote "A Victim of Justice" in early 1895 and that he combined in the story his memory of the January, 1894, lynching, his July, 1894, article (from which he quoted several passages verbatim), and his visit to Missouri in the summer of 1894.

The next extant version of the story is a manuscript in the Los Angeles Public Library entitled "The Lynching of Nigger Jeff." This manuscript served, with minor changes, as the text for the November, 1901, publication of "Nigger Jeff" in *Ainslee's Magazine*. Encouraged by his friend Arthur Henry, Dreiser had begun writing stories in earnest during the summer of 1899, and he later recalled that "Nigger Jeff"—that is, the Los Angeles Public Library-*Ainslee's* version—dates from this period.[5] The fourth version of the story is Dreiser's revision of the *Ainslee's* version for inclusion in his *Free and Other Stories*, published in August, 1918. Since the changes in this last version are primarily additions to the *Ainslee's* text, and since this added material is not in the Los Angeles Public Library manuscript, the revision can be at-

tributed to the period shortly before the appearance of *Free*,
when Dreiser collected and revised his stories for republication.[6]

There are thus three major versions of "Nigger Jeff." Although none of these versions can be dated exactly, each can
be associated with an important segment of Dreiser's career.
The Virginia manuscript of the mid-1890s reflects the Dreiser depicted in *A Book About Myself*, the young journalist who
was viewing much of the tragic complexity of life but understanding little of it. The *Ainslee's* publication represents the
Dreiser of *Sister Carrie*. The story has been rewritten by an author with a characteristic vision of life and with a distinctive
fictional style. The 1918 publication suggests a writer whose
ideas have become increasingly self-conscious and polemical,
the Dreiser of the essays of *Hey Rub-a-Dub-Dub* (1920) and the
Dreiser who was eventually to devote a large portion of his
later career to philosophical inquiries. The three versions, in
short, span the principal periods of Dreiser's career, and
their differences can tell us much about Dreiser's developing
aesthetic.

Although the three versions of "Nigger Jeff" differ in a
number of important ways, all have the same basic outline. A
young man is sent in early spring to investigate reports of a
possible lynching in a rural Missouri community.[7] He discovers that a farmer's daughter has been attacked by a Negro
and that the farmer and his son are in pursuit of the Negro in
order to lynch him. The Negro is apprehended by a local
peace officer, however, and is taken to another village for
safekeeping until the arrival of reinforcements. A mob gath-
ers, overpowers the peace officer, and returns with the Negro
to its own community, where he is hanged from a bridge. The
following day the investigator visits the home of the Negro
and views his body.

Dreiser's earliest version of this story, "A Victim of Justice," is told in the first person and uses a frame device. The story opens with the unidentified narrator visiting a Potter's Field near a small Missouri town. After much soulful lament over the "strange exigencies of life" that have brought the denizens of the graveyard to their mournful fate, the narrator is disturbed by the "grieving orisons" of an elderly woman. Before he can question her, she departs. But she has stimulated still further his moody reflections on the "wounding trials of life," and it is on this note that he introduces his recollections of the lynching. He begins by explaining that he was "commissioned to examine into the details" of the incident, but he does not identify himself as a reporter. Nor do we have a sense of his involvement in the action of the story. His narrative "voice" is principally an omniscient authorial voice, telling us about the lynching (often in summary form) but devoid of personal participation. The story concludes with the second half of the frame device. The narrator describes the Negro's lonely grave on a hillside, a burial place marked by a wooden cross. "Day after day it stands, bleak, gray, desolate, a fitting emblem of the barren life now forgotten, wasted as sparks are wasted on the night wind." Again the narrator broods over the vicissitudes of life, though his melancholy is lightened somewhat by the thought that nature is ever-beautiful even in this forsaken spot.

"A Victim of Justice" has three major themes. The first is suggested by the ironic title of the story and by several authorial comments. The Negro (named Jim in this version) is the victim of the "hasty illegalities" and "summary justice" of the mob. The second theme involves a more generalized sorrow over the fate of most men, a theme which arises out of the narrator's "meditations" in the graveyard. Dreiser's lugubrious exploitation of the conventional rhetoric of injustice and melancholy suggests that both themes have their source in the traditional literature of sentiment. Jim is a "poor varlet," and the graveyard scene echoes the diction and sentence structure of a Hawthorne or an Irving. Life is sad, Dreiser says, and he asks us to share this sentiment by imitating the prose of writers known for their ability to evoke melancholic moods. The third theme of the story is that of the powerful human emotions that arise out of the lynching itself—the quest for vengeance by the father, the resoluteness of the peace officer, the terror of the Negro. In a sense these emotions constitute a suppressed or unacknowledged theme, since they are extraneous to the explicit themes imposed upon the story by the narrator. The peace officer could have been a coward and Jim brave and unflinching, and the narrator would still have been able to enclose the story within his reflections on injustice and melancholy. These reflections may be apt responses to a lynching, but Dreiser's failure to integrate them into the account of the lynching itself implies that he has indeed imposed them on his response. His "true" response is "buried" within the narrative of the lynching, for Dreiser at this point was unable to articulate his response— that is, he was unable to recognize what moved him in the lynching. Thus, though he depicted the lynching as a moving event, he confused the nature of his response with those "deep" emotions readily available to him in traditional literary forms.

The *Ainslee's* version of "Nigger Jeff" omits the frame sections. The story, now told in the third person, focuses on the experiences of a young reporter, Eugene Davies,[8] who has been sent to look into a possible lynching. It is a beautiful spring day and the insouciant, self-confident Davies undertakes his assignment with relish. Arriving in Pleasant Valley, he is drawn into the events of the lynching as he pursues his story. Davies is at first a passive observer of these events. But when the blubbering, terrified Jeff is seized by the mob, the reporter uncontrollably "clapped his hands over his mouth and worked his fingers convulsively."[9] "Sick at heart" (373), he accompanies the mob back to Pleasant Valley. The hanging itself stuns him into a deep torpor. By the close of the story, when he encounters Jeff's weeping mother, he has viewed a wide range of character and emotion—the competent, strong-willed sheriff, the cowardly mob, the father intent on vengeance, and above all the terrified Jeff and his heartbroken mother.

In "A Victim of Justice" Dreiser mentioned the grieving mother early in the narrative but not afterward. In "Nigger Jeff" he reserved introducing her grief until the final, climactic scene of the story, a scene which is present only in brief summary form in the earlier version. As Davies views Jeff's body, he hears a noise in the room.

Greatly disturbed, he hesitated, and then as his eyes strained he caught the shadow of something. It was in the extreme corner, huddled up, dark, almost indistinguishable crouching against the cold walls.

"Oh, oh, oh," was repeated, even more plaintively than before.

Davies began to understand. He approached lightly. Then he made out an old black mammy, doubled up and weeping. She was in the very niche of the corner, her head sunk on her knees, her tears falling, her body rocking to and fro. (375)

On leaving the cabin, Davies "swelled with feeling and pathos. . . . The night, the tragedy, the grief, he saw it all.

" 'I'll get that in,' he exclaimed, feelingly, 'I'll get it all in' " (375).

Dreiser has thus shifted the axis of the story. Unlike "A Victim of Justice," in which the narrator presents us with a response to a lynching, "Nigger Jeff" dramatizes a growth in emotional responsiveness by the principal viewer of the action. The narrative is now primarily an initiation story—the coming into knowledge of the tragic realities of life by the viewer. And since the viewer is a reporter who will attempt to "get it all in," the story is also the dramatization of the birth of an aesthetic.

Briefly, the conception of the theme and form of art symbolized by the "it" in the last sentence of "Nigger Jeff" contains three major elements, each rendered in dramatic form within the story. These are: a belief that two emotions in particular pervade all life; a belief that these emotions are often found in moral and social contexts which lend them a special poignancy; and a belief that these emotions adopt a certain pattern in life and therefore in art. Let me discuss each of these beliefs more fully, beginning with the central emotions of life as Dreiser depicts them in this story.

One such emotion is sexual desire. It is the first flush of spring, and Jeff, a poor, ignorant Negro, attacks a white girl—a girl who knows him and whom he meets in a lane. " 'Before God, boss, I didn't mean to. . . . I didn't go to do it,' " he cries to the mob (372). Although sexual desire may not lead to the destruction of such figures as Frank Cowperwood, it is nevertheless a dominant, uncontrollable force in almost all of Dreiser's principal male characters. Hurstwood, Lester Kane, Eugene Witla, and Clyde Griffiths are at its mercy. In addition, the "it" of the final sentence includes the unthinking love and loyalty which exist within a family and particularly between a mother and a child. When Davies arrives at Jeff's home after the lynching, he asks the Negro's sister why Jeff had returned to his cabin, where he had been captured by the waiting sheriff.

"To see us," said the girl.

"Well, did he want anything? He didn't come just to see you, did he?"

"Yes, suh," said the girl, "he come to say good-by."

Her voice wavered.

"Didn't he know he might get caught?" asked Davies.

"Yes, suh, I think he did."

She stood very quietly, holding the poor battered lamp up, and looking down.

"Well, what did he have to say?" asked Davies.

"He said he wanted tuh see motha'. He was a-goin' away." (374)

The son come back to say good-by to the mother, the mother mourning over the son's body—here is emotion which in its over-powering intensity parallels the sex drive itself. It is the force which binds the Gerhardt family together, which is the final refuge of Clyde Griffiths, and which creates the tragic tension of Solon Barnes's loss of his children. In "Nigger Jeff" this force appears not only in the relationship between Jeff and his mother but also in the figure of the assaulted girl's father. Although Dreiser depicts the mob as cowardly and sensation-seeking, he respects the motives of the father. Both victim and revenger are caught up in the same inexplicable emotional oneness which is a family.

"Nigger Jeff" thus contains two of the most persistent themes in all of Dreiser's work—the power of desire and the power of family love and loyalty. Davies's awakening to their reality can be interpreted as Dreiser's declaration of belief in the dominance of these emotions in human affairs. Indeed, in his later autobiographies Dreiser depicted these emotions as two of the principal inner realities of his own youth. His ability to identify himself with these emotions as early as "Nigger Jeff" is revealed by a sentence omitted in *Ainslee's* but present in the Los Angeles Public Library manuscript of "The Lynching of Nigger Jeff." Immediately following "The night, the tragedy, the grief, he saw it all," there appears in "The Lynching of Nigger Jeff": "It was spring no less than sorrow that ran whispering in his blood." The sensuality of youth, the family love taking its shape in sorrow—these appear in Dreiser's work as complementary autobiographical themes until they coalesce most fully and powerfully both in *Dawn* and in *An American Tragedy*.

The second major aspect of Dreiser's aesthetic contained in the final "it" involves the moral and social context in which these emotions are found. Like most of Dreiser's characters, the principal figures in "Nigger Jeff" have little of the heroic about them. Even the sheriff loses his potential for such a role once he is easily tricked by the mob and complacently accepts its victory. Jeff himself is described at the moment of his capture by the mob as a "groveling, foaming brute" (372). But the major figures in "Nigger Jeff," despite their often grotesque inadequacies, feel and suffer, and the young reporter comes to realize the "tragedy" of their fate. To Dreiser, tragedy arises out of the realities that nature is beautiful, that man can desire, and that a mother or father can mourn. These realities do not lend "nobility" to Dreiser's figures; like Jeff, they are often weak and comtemptible despite their fate. But their capacity to feel combined with their incapacity to act wisely or well is to Dreiser the very stuff of man's tragic nature. The realization which the young reporter must "get in" thus involves not only the truths of lust and of mother love but also the truth that the experience of these emotions gives meaning and poignancy to every class and condition of man.

The third aspect of the aesthetic symbolized by the final "it" concerns the pattern assumed by the two principal emotions of the story. Most of Dreiser's novels involve a seeker or quester—sometimes driven by desire, sometimes by other motives—who finds at the end of the novel that he has returned to where he started: Carrie still seeking beauty and happiness; Jennie once again alone despite her immense capacity to love; Cowperwood's millions gone; Clyde still walled in; Solon returning to the simplicity of faith. It is possible to visualize Dreiser's novels as a graphic irony—the characters believe they are pushing forward but they are really moving in a circle. Dreiser occasionally makes this structural principle explicit by a consciously circular symbol, such as the rocking chair in *Sister Carrie* and the street scene in *An American Tragedy*. "Nigger Jeff" contains a rough approximation of this pattern. The passions which have driven the narrative forward in its sequence of crime and punishment are dissipated, and Jeff returns to where he has started both physically and emotionally. That is, the bleak room in which he rests and his mother keening over his body represent the permanent realities of his life and his death. He, too, has come full circle.

Despite his reputation as stylistically inept, Dreiser was capable of a provocative and moving verbal symbolism. This quality appears in his use of "beauty" in connection with Carrie at the close of *Sister Carrie* and in his use of "life" in the next to last paragraph of *The Bulwark* (" 'I am crying for *life*' "). These otherwise banal abstractions represent the complexity and depth of experience depicted in the novels concerned, and they are therefore powerfully evocative. The word "it" at the close of "Nigger Jeff" has some of the same quality. The word symbolizes a deeply felt aesthetic which Dreiser never explained as well elsewhere, just as he never discussed "beauty" and "life" in his philosophical writings as well as he dramatized their meaning for him in his novels.

The *Free* version of "Nigger Jeff" omits almost nothing from the *Ainslee's* text. Aside from stylistic revisions, the changes in the *Free* version consist of additions, many of which merely flesh out particular scenes. Some of the additions, however, extend the themes of the story in two significant ways.

One such extension is revealed in Dreiser's addition to the first sentence of the story (here and elsewhere the added material appears in brackets):

The city editor was waiting for one of his best reporters, Elmer Davies [by name, a vain and rather self-sufficient youth who was inclined to be of that turn of mind which sees in life only a fixed and ordered process of rewards and punishments. If one did not do exactly right, one did not get along well. On the contrary, if one did, one did. Only the so-called evil were really punished, only the good truly rewarded—or Mr. Davies had heard this so long in his youth that he had come nearly to believe it.][10]

By the next to last paragraph of the story, Davies has come to realize that "[it was not always exact justice that was meted out to all and that it was not so much the business of the writer to indict as to interpret]" (111). In these and similar additions Dreiser has extended the nature of Davies's initiation. In the *Ainslee's* version, Davies's growth is above all that of his awakening to the tragic nature of human experience. The *Free* version associates this awakening with his conscious awareness that moral absolutes are based on naivete or inexperience and are inapplicable to the complex realities of life. In a sense even "A Victim of Justice" contains an aspect of this theme, since Dreiser in that version noted the injustice of the "summary justice" of mob rule. But in the *Free* "Nigger Jeff" this theme is both more overt and more central. Its presence in this enlarged and emphatic form suggests Dreiser's increasing tendency throughout the later stages of his career (beginning about 1911) to associate the function of art with the explicit inversion of conventional moral and social beliefs. It is during this period that Dreiser the polemicist (as revealed in *Hey Rub-a-Dub-Dub*) and Dreiser the novelist combine to produce *An American Tragedy*, in which the putative reader is placed in the position of Davies. Like the naive beliefs of Davies, the reader's faith in the American dream of success and in the workings of justice is destroyed by encountering the reality of a tragedy.

A second major extension of theme in the *Free* "Nigger Jeff" occurs in the scenes following the capture of Jeff by the mob. As Davies accompanies the mob on its way to hang Jeff, he reflects that "[both father and son now seemed brutal, the injury to the daughter and sister not so vital as all this. Still, also, custom seemed to require death in this way for this. It was like some axiomatic, mathematic law—hard, but custom. The silent company, an articulated, mechanical and therefore terrible thing, moved on. It also was axiomatic, mathematic]" (103). After the hanging, Davies sits near the bridge and muses: "[Life seemed so sad, so strange, so mysterious, so inexplicable]" (105). These additions reflect two of the principal areas of Dreiser's philosophical speculation during the last half of his career. On the one hand, he believed that every phase of life is governed by law. During the period from approximately 1910 to the late 1920s he often, as in the *Free* "Nigger Jeff," associated this law with the harsh extermination of the weak. Dreiser the mechanist called this law an "equation inevitable" in *Hey Rub-a-Dub-Dub*. But by the end of his career Dreiser the quasi pantheist had come to call it "design" in *The Bulwark* and to associate it primarily with beauty and with cosmic benevolence. His particular conception of law at various stages of his later career, however, is perhaps less important than his enduring search for a principle of meaning which would encompass the cruelty and the beauty, the destructiveness and the continuity, which he found in life. On the other hand, Dreiser affirmed throughout his later career a belief in the essential mystery at the heart of life. Both attitudes—the search for meaning and the belief in mystery—are present in *Hey Rub-a-Dub-Dub*, in which the often doctrinaire mechanistic philosophizing is counterbalanced by the subtitle of the work: "A Book of the Mystery and Wonder and Terror of Life." And both are present in *The Bulwark*, in which Solon's discovery of the principle of design is inseparable from his discovery of the mystery of life. In his *Free* version of "Nigger Jeff" Dreiser has thus expanded his aesthetic to include not only an explicit ironic reversal of moral certainties but also a dramatization of the vast philosophical paradoxes underlying all life. Davies's discovery of what art must do—"[to interpret]"—now has a conscious philosophical element which was to play an ever increasing role in Dreiser's career.

The various versions of "Nigger Jeff" which I have been discussing incorporate Dreiser's principal beliefs about the nature of art. From the imposed sentimentality of "A Victim of Justice" to the moral polemicism and incipient philosophizing of the *Free* "Nigger Jeff," the three versions reflect much that is central in Dreiser's thought and in his practice as a writer. No doubt there is room for qualification of some of the generalizations about Dreiser's developing aesthetic which I have drawn from this study of the three versions of "Nigger Jeff." Nevertheless, there is much to be said for the attempt to deduce a writer's beliefs about art directly from a creative work dealing with the nature of art rather than from his literary criticism. For Dreiser, there is a special need for this kind of attempt, since most of his overt comments about art are either vague or overpolemical. Moreover, we have come to realize that Dreiser is not only a writer of stature (as Alfred Kazin maintained) but also of finesse (as Ellen Moers believed).[11] He is a writer, in other words, whose stories and novels in their various revisions can often be explored for the complex intertwining of permanence and change characteristic of the creative work of a major literary figure.

Notes

Bibliography

Index

Notes

1—Late Nineteenth-Century American Realism

1. "Realism: An Essay in Definition," 10 (June 1949): 184–97; expanded and revised into "Modern Realism as a Literary Movement," *Documents of Modern Literary Realism*, ed. George J. Becker (Princeton: Princeton Univ. Pr., 1963), pp. 3–38. For other significant efforts to define American literary realism, see Harold H. Kolb, Jr., *The Illusion of Life: American Realism as a Literary Form* (Charlottesville: Univ. Pr. of Virginia, 1969) and Edwin H. Cady, *The Light of Common Day: Realism in American Fiction* (Bloomington: Indiana Univ. Pr., 1971).
2. Although Becker actually divides realism into three categories (the realistic mode, realism of subject matter, and philosophical realism), I have confined my discussion to the first. He notes of the second category that it is "no more than an outgrowth and extension of the first, but it is so important that we should disengage it and look at it separately, calling it realism of subject matter." He defines the third category as "pessimistic determinism" or naturalism, "a philosophical position taken by some realists." I discuss this third category in my essay on naturalism.

2—Late Nineteenth-Century American Naturalism

1. Richard Chase, *The American Novel and Its Tradition* (Garden City, N.Y.: Doubleday, 1957), p. 186n; George J. Becker, "Modern Realism as a Literary Movement," in *Documents of Modern Literary Realism*, ed. George J. Becker (Princeton: Princeton Univ. Pr., 1963), p. 35. See also the definitions by Lars Ahnebrink, *The Beginnings of Naturalism in American Fiction* (Cambridge: Harvard Univ. Pr., 1950), pp. vi–vii; Malcolm Cowley, "A Natural History of American Naturalism," *Documents*, pp. 429–30; and Philip Rahv, "Notes on the Decline of Naturalism," *Documents*, pp. 583–84.

2. The discussion of naturalism in the next two paragraphs resembles in several ways that by Charles C. Walcutt in his *American Literary Naturalism, A Divided Stream* (Minneapolis: Univ. of Minnesota Pr., 1956), pp. 3–29. In general, I accept Walcutt's analysis of naturalism's philosophical and literary ambivalences. I believe, however, that his discussion of the naturalists' divided view of nature and of their maintenance of the idea of free will by implicitly encouraging their readers to social action are ways of describing these ambivalences historically and socially—by source and effect—rather than as they function within the naturalistic novel itself.

3. Erich Auerbach's *Mimesis: The Representation of Reality in Western Literature* (Princeton: Princeton Univ. Pr., 1953) deals with the representation of these ideas in imaginative literature from antiquity to our own day.

4. Frank Norris, "A Plea for Romantic Fiction," *The Literary Criticism of Frank Norris*, ed. Donald Pizer (Austin: Univ. of Texas Pr., 1964), p. 77.

5. *McTeague*, ed. Donald Pizer (New York: Norton, 1977), p. 177. Citations hereafter appear in the text.

6. I discuss this aspect of Norris's thought at some length in my "Evolutionary Ethical Dualism in Frank Norris' *Vandover and the Brute* and *McTeague*," *PMLA*, 76 (Dec. 1961): 522–60.

7. Lionel Trilling, "Reality in America," *The Liberal Imagination* (New York: Viking, 1950).

8. *Sister Carrie*, ed. Donald Pizer (New York: Norton, 1970), p. 367.
9. See William A. Freedman, "A Look at Dreiser as Artist: The Motif of Circularity in *Sister Carrie*," *Modern Fiction Studies*, 8 (Winter 1962-63): 384-92 and my own "Nineteenth-Century American Naturalism: An Approach Through Form" which follows.
10. *The Red Badge of Courage*, ed. Donald Pizer (New York: Norton, 2nd rev. ed., 1976), p. 33. Citations hereafter appear in the text.

3—American Literary Naturalism: An Approach Through Form

1. Edwin H. Cady, *The Light of Common Day: Realism in American Fiction* (Bloomington: Indiana Univ. Pr., 1971), p. 45.
2. For other views of the naturalistic symbol and the form of the naturalistic novel, see Charles C. Walcutt, *American Literary Naturalism, A Divided Stream* (Minneapolis: Univ. of Minnesota Pr., 1956); Robert M. Figg, "Naturalism as a Literary Form," *Georgia Review*, 18 (Fall 1964): 308-16; and Frederick J. Hoffman, "From Document to Symbol: Zola and American Naturalism," *Revue des Langues Vivantes*, U. S. Bicentennial Issue (1976): 203-12.
3. Richard Ellmann, *James Joyce* (New York: Oxford Univ. Pr., 1959), p. 3.

4—American Literary Naturalism: The Example of Dreiser

1. Quoted by Franklin Walker, *Frank Norris: A Biography* (Garden City, N.Y.: Doubleday, Doran, 1932), pp. 222-23.
2. The most characteristic discussions of American naturalism occur in histories of American fiction. See, for example, Harry Hartwick, *The Foreground of American Fiction* (New York: American, 1934), pp. 3-20; George Snell, *The Shapers of American Fic-*

tion, 1798–1947 (New York: Dutton, 1947), pp. 223–48; Frederick J. Hoffman, *The Modern Novel in America* (Chicago: Regnery, 1951), pp. 28–51; and Edward Wagenknecht, *Cavalcade of the American Novel* (New York: Holt, 1952), pp. 204–29. But see also Oscar Cargill, *Intellectual America* (New York: Macmillan, 1941), pp. 82–175, and Lars Ahnebrink, *The Beginnings of Naturalism in American Fiction* (Cambridge: Harvard Univ. Pr., 1950).

3. Charles C. Walcutt, *American Literary Naturalism, A Divided Stream* (Minneapolis: Univ. of Minnesota Pr., 1956), p. 220.

4. Eliseo Vivas, "Dreiser, An Inconsistent Mechanist," *Ethics* (July 1938); revised version, *The Stature of Theodore Dreiser*, ed. Alfred Kazin and Charles Shapiro (Bloomington: Indiana Univ. Pr., 1955), p. 237.

5. Two extreme examples of this position are Randall Stewart, *American Literature and Christian Doctrine* (Baton Rouge: Louisiana State Univ. Pr., 1958), pp. 114–20, and Floyd Stovall, *American Idealism* (Norman: Univ. of Oklahoma Pr., 1943), pp. 134–36.

6. The essays were published originally in 1942, 1947, and 1950 respectively.

7. See, for example, Charles Thomas Samuels, "Mr. Trilling, Mr. Warren, and *An American Tragedy*," *Yale Review*, 53 (Summer 1964): 629–40. Samuels finds *An American Tragedy* inept beyond belief.

8. *Sister Carrie*, ed. Donald Pizer (New York: Norton, 1970), p. 56.

9. Portions of the discussion of *Jennie Gerhardt* and *An American Tragedy* which follows appear in different form in my *The Novels of Theodore Dreiser: A Critical Study* (Minneapolis: Univ. of Minnesota Pr., 1976). I do not wish by my emphasis on the deterministic thread in naturalism to appear to be supporting a return to a simplistic definition of naturalism as "pessimistic determinism" or some such formula. I have devoted much effort over two decades in various critical studies of individual naturalists as well as in more general essays on the movement as a whole to the position that naturalism is a complex literary movement in which distinctive writers combine in their works

distinctive strains of traditional humanistic values and contemporary deterministic belief. Rather, I seek in this essay to suggest that just as we were long guilty of not recognizing the element of covertly expressed traditional value in most naturalists, so we have also been guilty of an uncritical disparagement of the more readily identifiable deterministic strain in their work.

10. *Jennie Gerhardt* (New York: Harper, 1911), p. 401. Citations appear hereafter in the text.
11. In the Theodore Dreiser Collection, University of Pennsylvania Library; quoted by permission of the University of Pennsylvania Library.
12. *An American Tragedy* (New York: Boni and Liveright, 1925), I, 5. Citations appear hereafter in the text.

5—The Problem of Philosophy in the Naturalistic Novel

1. *Vandover and the Brute* (Garden City, N.Y.: Doubleday, Page, 1914), pp. 230–31.
2. Fuller discussions of Norris's ideas about art in *Vandover* can be found in my *The Novels of Frank Norris* (Bloomington: Indiana Univ. Pr., 1966), pp. 23–52 and Don Graham, *The Fiction of Frank Norris: The Aesthetic Context* (Columbia: Univ. of Missouri Pr., 1978), pp. 16–42.
3. *Sister Carrie*, ed. Donald Pizer (New York: Norton, 1970), pp. 56–57.
4. *Sister Carrie*, p. 24.

6—The Evolutionary Foundation of W. D. Howells's *Criticism and Fiction*

1. See Herbert Edwards, "Howells and the Controversy over Realism in American Fiction," *American Literature*, 3 (Nov. 1931): 237–48, and Leonard Lutwack, "William Dean Howells and the 'Editor's Study,' " *American Literature*, 24 (May 1952): 195–207.

2. *Howells and the Age of Realism* (Philadelphia: Lippincott 1954), p. 190. See also Robert P. Falk, "The Literary Criticism of the Genteel Decades: 1870–1900," *The Development of American Literary Criticism*, ed. Floyd Stovall (Chapel Hill: Univ. of North Carolina Pr., 1955), p. 137.

3. *Howells and the Age of Realism*, p. 190.

4. Three surveys of evolutionary criticism are: Harry H. Clark, "The Influence of Science on American Literary Criticism, 1860–1910 . . .," *Transactions of the Wisconsin Academy of Sciences, Arts and Letters*, 44 (1955): 109–64; René Wellek, "The Concept of Evolution in Literary History," *Concepts of Criticism* (New Haven: Yale Univ. Pr., 1963), pp. 37–53; and Thomas Munro, "Evolutionary Theories of Literature," *Evolution in the Arts* (Cleveland: Cleveland Museum of Art, 1963), pp. 145–52.

5. For a descriptive analysis of this work, see Donald Pizer, *Hamlin Garland's Early Work and Career* (Berkeley and Los Angeles: Univ. of California Pr., 1960), pp. 13–21.

6. *Hamlin Garland's Early Work*, pp. 17–18.

7. *Hamlin Garland's Early Work*, pp. 18–19.

8. Herbert Spencer, *First Principles* (New York: Appleton, 1886 [1864]), p. 517. Faith in progress was, of course, a traditional American belief, but in the late nineteenth century it found renewed support in the evolutionary philosophy of Herbert Spencer. See Richard Hofstadter, *Social Darwinism in American Thought, 1860–1915* (Philadelphia: Univ. of Pennsylvania Pr., 1945), pp. 18–36.

9. (New York: Appleton, 1886), p. [v]. Posnett was educated at Cambridge, was associated with Trinity College, Dublin, and from 1886 was Professor of Classics and English Literature at University College, Auckland, New Zealand. For a summary of his position and an account of its derivation, see his "The Science of Comparative Literature," *Contemporary Review*, 79 (1901): 855–72.

10. *Comparative Literature*, p. 20.

11. (New York: Harper, 1883), p. vi.

12. *English Literature*, p. ix. The relationship between the genius (or great man) and evolutionary progress was much discussed in the eighties. See Philip P. Wiener, *Evolution and the Founders of Pragmatism* (Cambridge: Harvard Univ. Pr., 1949), pp. 129–36.

13. Perry, *English Literature*, p. ix.
14. For Perry and Symonds, see Virginia Harlow, *Thomas Sergeant Perry: A Biography* (Durham, N.C.: Duke Univ. Pr., 1950), pp. 103–5, 119–21.
15. Perry, *A History of Greek Literature* (New York: Holt, 1890), p. 297. Although not published until 1890, this work was completed in 1885. See Harlow, *T. S. Perry*, p. 139.
16. See particularly Harry H. Clark, "The Role of Science in the Thought of W. D. Howells," *Transactions of the Wisconsin Academy of Sciences, Arts and Letters*, 42 (1953): 263–303; also Carter, *Howells and the Age of Realism*, pp. 91–102, and Edwin H. Cady, *The Road to Realism* (Syracuse: Syracuse Univ. Pr., 1956), pp. 147–51.
17. For an account of the close literary and personal relationship between Howells and Perry, see Virginia Harlow, "William Dean Howells and Thomas Sergeant Perry," *Boston Public Library Quarterly*, 1 (Oct. 1949): 135–50. Howells wrote to Perry on March 3, 1886, that he had told a friend "that *I had learned from you* the new and true way of looking at literature." *Life in Letters of William Dean Howells*, ed. Mildred Howells (Garden City, N.Y.: Doubleday, Doran, 1928), I, 379. Howells became aware of Garland's critical ideas when the two men met in the summer of 1887.
18. *Harper's Monthly*, 73 (July 1886): 318.
19. *Harper's Monthly*, 74 (Dec. 1886): 161–62 and 82 (Apr. 1891): pp. 803–4.
20. *Criticism and Fiction* (New York: Harper, 1891), pp. 1–2. Citations hereafter appear in the text.

7—Evolutionary Ideas in Late Nineteenth-Century English and American Literary Criticism

1. See Morse Peckham, "Darwinism and Darwinisticism," *Victorian Studies*, 3 (Sept. 1959): 19–40, for an explanation of the relatively negligible influence of the theory of natural selection. In terms of Peckham's definitions, the evolutionary ideas which I discuss are for the most part "Darwinisticistic"—that is, they

owe less to the theory of natural selection than to other ideas of emergence and development which were popularized or introduced as a result of the impact of Darwinism.

2. *Comparative Literature* (New York: Appleton, 1886), p. 20.

3. "The Philosophy of Evolution," *Essays Speculative and Suggestive* (New York: Scribner's, 1907 [1890]), p. 5.

4. "On the Application of Evolutionary Principles to Art and Literature," *Essays*, p. 28.

5. See Donald Pizer, *Hamlin Garland's Early Work and Career* (Berkeley and Los Angeles: Univ. of California Pr., 1960), pp. 13–21.

6. *From Opitz to Lessing: A Study of Pseudo-Classicism in Literature* (Boston: Osgood, 1885), pp. 143–44.

7. "American Literary Criticism and the Doctrine of Evolution," *International Monthly*, 2 (Aug. 1900): 153.

8. "The Evolution of American Thought," quoted by Pizer, *Hamlin Garland's Early Work*, pp. 17–18.

9. "American Literary Criticism and the Doctrine of Evolution," *International Monthly*, 2 (July 1900): 41.

10. Symonds, "On the Application of Evolutionary Principles to Art and Literature," *Essays*, pp. 27–52; Perry, *A History of Greek Literature* (New York: Holt, 1890), p. 859; and "The Progress of Literature," *Gately's World's Progress*, ed. Charles E. Beale (Boston: Gately and Williams, 1886), p. 661.

11. *Criticism and Fiction* (New York: Harper, 1891), pp. 18–22, 119.

12. *Criticism and Fiction*, p. 24.

13. *A History of Greek Literature*, p. 297.

14. *From Opitz to Lessing*, p. 140.

15. *Criticism and Fiction*, p. 88.

16. See, for example, Payne, "American Literary Criticism," p. 40. The "spontaneous variation" conception of literary greatness was reinforced in the early twentieth century by De Vries's mutation theory.

17. *Crumbling Idols* (Chicago and Cambridge, Mass.: Stone and Kimball, 1894), p. 191.

18. "On the Application of Evolutionary Principles," *Essays*, p. 37.

19. "On Some Principles of Criticism," *Essays*, pp. 53–78.

20. *Criticism and Fiction*, p. 30.

21. *From Opitz to Lessing*, p. 58.

22. "The Scientific Movement and Literature," *Studies in Literature, 1789–1877* (London: Paul, Trench, Trübner, 1899 [1878]), p. 106.
23. "American Literary Criticism," p. 45.
24. "American Literary Criticism," p. 39.
25. *Comparative Literature*, p. 76.
26. "American Literary Criticism," p. 149.

8—Hamlin Garland and Stephen Crane: The Naturalist as Romantic Individualist

1. *The American Mind* (Boston: Houghton Mifflin, 1912), pp. 3–46. Cf. Richard D. Mosier, *The American Temper* (Berkeley: Univ. of Calif. Pr., 1952).
2. Garland, *Crumbling Idols* (Chicago and Cambridge, Mass.: Stone and Kimball, 1894), p. vii. Citations hereafter appear in the text.
3. See Philip P. Wiener, *Evolution and the Founders of Pragmatism* (Cambridge: Harvard Univ. Pr., 1949).
4. Eugène Véron, *Aesthetics*, trans. W. H. Armstrong (Philadelphia: Lippincott, 1879), p. [v]. This copy of Veron is in the Hamlin Garland Collection, University of Southern California Library. All unpublished material cited hereafter is in the University of Southern California Library. I wish to thank Mrs. Constance Garland Doyle for permission to quote from Garland's unpublished work, and the University of Southern California Library for permission to consult its Hamlin Garland Collection.
5. Véron, p. xv.
6. Véron, p. xxii. Sometime during October–November, 1886, Garland copied this passage into his Mar. 3, 1886 notebook ("Literary Notes. Vol. I" on spine; "March 3/86" on flyleaf).
7. Véron, p. 369.
8. In Garland's Mar. 3, 1886, notebook, shortly after a sketch dated Mar. 20, 1887.
9. "Ibsen as a Dramatist," *Arena*, 2 (June 1890): 77.

10. When originally published in "Literary Emancipation of the West," *Forum*, 16 (Oct. 1893), 166, this passage was directed specifically at Western authors. It began, "Stand up, O young man and woman of the West!" and it also called upon Western writers to "Reject the scholasticism of the East." In *Crumbling Idols*, however, the passage was taken out of context to serve in the "Recapitulatory After-Word" where Garland clearly wished to broaden the range of his plea.

11. *Stephen Crane: An Omnibus*, ed. R. W. Stallman (New York: Knopf, 1952), p. xix.

12. See Marcus Cunliffe, "Stephen Crane and the American Background of *Maggie*," *American Quarterly*, 7 (Spring 1955): 31–44.

13. *Stephen Crane: Letters*, ed. R. W. Stallman and Lillian Gilkes (New York: New York Univ. Pr , 1960), p. 14; hereafter referred to as *Letters*.

14. The program for the full schedule of lectures has been published by Lars Ahnebrink, *The Beginnings of Naturalism in American Fiction* (Cambridge: Harvard Univ. Pr., 1950), pp. 442–43.

15. "Howells Discussed at Avon-by-the-Sea," *New York Tribune*, Aug. 18, 1891, p. 5. Republished in *The Works of Stephen Crane*, ed. Fredson Bowers (Charlottesville: Univ. Pr. of Virginia, 1973), VIII, 507–8.

16. *Letters*, p. 62.

17. To Lily B. Munroe, Mar. 1894; *Letters*, p. 31.

18. William Dean Howells, *Criticism and Fiction* (New York: Harper, 1891), p. 145.

19. Letter to Miss Catherine Harris, Nov. 12, 1896; *Letters*, p. 133.

20. Letter to John N. Hilliard, Jan. 1896; *Letters*, p. 110.

9—Frank Norris's Definition of Naturalism

1. "A Plea for Romantic Fiction," *Boston Evening Transcript*, December 18, 1901, p. 14; "Zola as a Romantic Writer," *Wave*, 15 (June 27, 1896): 3; "Frank Norris' Weekly Letter," *Chicago*

American Literary Review, Aug. 3, 1901, p. 5. The first essay was republished in *The Responsibilities of the Novelist* (New York: Doubleday, Page, 1903); the second was partially reprinted in Franklin Walker, *Frank Norris: A Biography* (Garden City, N.Y.: Doubleday, Doran, 1932). The third essay was republished, along with the first two, in *The Literary Criticism of Frank Norris*, ed. Donald Pizer (Austin: Univ. of Texas Pr., 1964). Quotations refer to *The Literary Criticism of Frank Norris*.

2. "Zola as a Romantic Writer," p. 71.

3. "A Plea for Romantic Fiction," p. 76.

4. "A Plea for Romantic Fiction," p. 76.

5. "A Plea for Romantic Fiction," p. 78.

6. "Zola as a Romantic Writer," p. 72.

7. It was not uncommon throughout Zola's career for critics to call him a romanticist because of his sensational plots, though such critics usually intended disparagement rather than praise. See Max Nordau, *Degeneration* (New York: Appleton, 1895), pp. 494–97, and F. W. J. Hemmings, *Émile Zola* (Oxford: Clarendon Pr., 1953), p. 74.

8. "Frank Norris' Weekly Letter," p. 75.

9. This choice of novels is not entirely clear, but perhaps it can be explained by the contemporary reputation of the three works and by the fact Norris was writing for a newspaper supplement. *La Débâcle* was well received in America, while *La Terre* was attacked for its gross sexuality and *Fécondité* was heavily criticized for its excessive polemicism.

10. "Frank Norris' Weekly Letter," p. 75.

11. "Zola as a Romantic Writer," p. 72.

12. See Zola's *The Experimental Novel and Other Essays* (New York: Cassell, 1893), pp. 17–18, and Lars Ahnebrink, *The Beginnings of Naturalism in American Fiction* (Cambridge: Harvard Univ. Pr., 1950), pp. vi–vii; and Charles C. Walcutt, *American Literary Naturalism, A Divided Stream* (Minneapolis: Univ. of Minnesota Pr., 1956), pp. vii–viii.

13. Norris to Marcosson, November, 1899, in *The Letters of Frank Norris*, ed. Franklin Walker (San Francisco: Book Club of California, 1956), p. 48.

10—The Significance of Frank Norris's Literary Criticism

1. Franklin Walker, *Frank Norris: A Biography* (Garden City, N.Y.: Doubleday, Doran, 1932), pp. 1-5.
2. It should be clear that I use "primitivistic" in its cultural rather than chronological sense. Norris's primitivism establishes certain key values in nature; he does not claim that these values flourished more in the past than in the present.
3. See Jerome Buckley, *The Victorian Temper* (Cambridge: Harvard Univ. Pr., 1951) and William Gaunt, *The Aesthetic Adventure* (New York: Harcourt, Brace, 1945).
4. See Grant C. Knight, *The Critical Period in American Literature* (Chapel Hill: Univ. of North Carolina Pr., 1951), pp. 70-75.
5. Jerome Buckley, *William Ernest Henley: A Study in the "Counter-Decadence" of the 'Nineties* (Princeton: Princeton Univ. Pr., 1945).
6. See James D. Hart's Introduction to Gelett Burgess, *Bayside Bohemia: Fin de Siècle San Francisco and Its Little Magazines* (San Francisco: Book Club of California, 1954).
7. See "Frank Norris' Weekly Letter," *Chicago American*, August 24, 1901 and "New York as a Literary Center," syndicated January 19, 1902. The two articles are reprinted in *The Literary Criticism of Frank Norris*, ed. Donald Pizer (Austin: Univ. of Texas Pr., 1964), pp. 30-33, 36-40.
8. *Smart Set*, 7 (July 1902): 95-101. Citations in the text refer to the republication of the story in *The Complete Edition of Frank Norris* (Garden City, N.Y.: Doubleday, Doran, 1928), IV, 113-27.
9. "Frank Norris' Weekly Letter," *Chicago American*, June 8, 1901; reprinted in *The Literary Criticism of Frank Norris*, pp. 9-10.
10. For discussions of the literary expression of this faith, see Philip Rahv, "The Cult of Experience in American Writing," *Image and Idea* (Norfolk, Conn.: New Directions, 1949) and Lionel Trilling, "Reality in America," *The Liberal Imagination* (New York: Viking, 1950).

11—The Ethical Unity of *The Rise of Silas Lapham*

1. Among the best explications of the novel are those by George Arms, *The Rise of Silas Lapham* (New York: Rinehart, 1949), pp. v–xvi; Everett Carter, *Howells and the Age of Realism* (Philadelphia: Lippincott, 1954), pp. 164–69; Edwin H. Cady, *The Road to Realism* (Syracuse: Syracuse Univ. Pr., 1956), pp. 230–40; and George N. Bennett, *William Dean Howells: The Development of a Novelist* (Norman: Univ. of Oklahoma Pr., 1959), pp. 150–61. Since the initial publication of this essay, G. Thomas Tanselle has written a full account of the relationship between the two plots in the novel in his "The Architecture of *The Rise of Silas Lapham*," *American Literature*, 37 (Jan. 1966): 430–57.

2. *The Rise of Silas Lapham*, A Selected Edition of W. D. Howells (Bloomington: Indiana Univ. Pr., 1971), XII, 241. Citations hereafter appear in the text.

3. Although Howells hints that the agents are counterfeit rather than real Englishmen, I have followed him in designating them as English.

4. By the close of chapter 19 Irene has been told of Tom's preference, Lapham has given Tom permission to continue courting Penelope, and Penelope has indicated (in the final words of chapter 19) that it will only be a matter of time before she will accept Tom. The problem of the depreciated mill is introduced in the next chapter.

5. Mrs. Lapham's ethical values are a foil to those which Lapham ultimately practices. Her moral beliefs are strongly held but are fragmented; she is helpless and uncertain when a conflict of interests is presented and a universal moral criterion is needed.

6. See particularly Clara M. Kirk, *W. D. Howells, Traveler from Altruria, 1889–1894* (New Brunswick, N.J.: Rutgers Univ. Pr., 1962).

7. *Utilitarianism, Liberty, and Representative Government*, Everyman's Library (London: Dent, 1910), p. 16.

8. Cf. Mill, *Utilitarianism*, pp. 15–16. "The utilitarian morality does recognize in human beings the power of sacrificing their greatest good for the good of others. It only refuses to admit that the sacrifice is itself a good. A sacrifice which does not increase, or tend to increase, the sum of happiness, it considers as wasted. The only self-renunciation which it applauds, is devotion to the happiness, or to some of the means of happiness, of others; either of mankind collectively, or of individuals within the limits imposed by the collective interests of mankind."

9. Howells, *My Literary Passions* (New York: Harper, 1895), p. 251.

12—Hamlin Garland's 1891 *Main-Travelled Roads*: Local Color as Art

1. Alice Cary, *Clovernook* (1853); quoted by Henry Nash Smith, *Virgin Land: The American West as Symbol and Myth* (Cambridge: Harvard Univ. Pr., 1950), p. 231.

2. Quoted by Donald Pizer, *Hamlin Garland's Early Work and Career* (Berkeley and Los Angeles: Univ. of California Pr., 1960), pp. 35–36.

3. *Main-Travelled Roads: Six Mississippi Valley Stories* (Boston: Arena, 1891), p. 115; republished in facsimile, ed. Donald Pizer (Columbus, Ohio: Charles E. Merrill, 1970). Citations hereafter appear in the text.

4. *Hamlin Garland's Early Work*, p. 40.

5. See Donald Pizer, " 'John Boyle's Conclusion': An Unpublished Middle Border Story by Hamlin Garland," *American Literature*, 31 (Mar. 1959); 59–75.

6. *A Son of the Middle Border* (New York: Macmillan, 1917), p. 415.

7. Garland's idea of the nature of aesthetic and social superiority, however, often reflects his relative inexperience in these matters. Will's promise to Agnes of sunshine on the Bay of Naples and Howard's memories of his yachts are derivative and forced images of such superiority.

13—Stephen Crane's Maggie and American Naturalism

1. Both R. W. Stallman, in "Crane's *Maggie*: A Reassessment," *Modern Fiction Studies*, 5 (Autumn 1959): 251–59, and Charles C. Walcutt, in *American Literary Naturalism, A Divided Stream* (Minneapolis: Univ. of Minnesota Pr., 1956), pp. 67–72, touch briefly on the theme of *Maggie* somewhat as I do. I have also been aided by Edwin H. Cady, *Stephen Crane* (Boston: Twayne, 1980), pp. 104–13; Joseph X. Brennan, "Ironic and Symbolic Structure in Crane's *Maggie*," *Nineteenth-Century Fiction*, 16 (March 1962): 303–15; and Janet Overmyer. "The Structure of Crane's *Maggie*," *University of Kansas City Review*, 29 (Autumn 1962): 71–72.
2. Stephen Crane, *Maggie: A Girl of the Streets* (New York, 1893); facsimile ed., ed. Donald Pizer (San Francisco: Chandler, 1968), p. [3]. Citations hereafter appear in the text.
3. *Stephen Crane: Letters*, ed. R. W. Stallman and Lillian Gilkes (New York: New York Univ. Pr., 1960), p. 14.

14—Synthetic Criticism and Frank Norris's The Octopus

1. *Massachusetts Review*, 1 (Oct. 1959): 62–95. This essay appears in somewhat revised form in Marx's *The Machine in the Garden* (New York: Oxford Univ. Pr., 1964).
2. My italics.
3. *The Economic Novel in America* (Chapel Hill: Univ. of North Carolina Pr., 1942), p. 325.
4. The first two paragraphs of the following discussion of *The Octopus* summarize the thesis of my "The Concept of Nature in Frank Norris' *The Octopus*," *American Quarterly*, 14 (Spring 1962): 73–80.
5. *The Complete Edition of Frank Norris* (Garden City, N.Y.: Doubleday, Doran, 1928), II, 343. Citations hereafter appear in the text.

6. This theme is even more explicit in *The Pit*, where the two opposing groups (the bulls and the bears) are similar, despite their antagonism, because both use the need for wheat as a means of speculative gain. *The Pit* also contains a more elaborate and simplified discussion of the omnipotence of the law of supply and demand in determining the production of wheat, an idea dramatized in *The Octopus* but introduced explicitly only briefly by Shelgrim. These few remarks of Shelgrim's, all of which derive from his idea that " 'Where there is a demand sooner or later there will be a supply' " (II, 285), have caused much anguish among readers of the novel, since Presley appears to be wholly convinced by Shelgrim's defense of the railroad as but " 'a force born out of certain conditions.' " What such readers fail to recognize is that within the context of the novel Shelgrim's use of the law of supply and demand as a defense of the railroad's practices is contravened in two major ways. First, the punishment of Behrman suggests that men are responsible for evil acts committed while participating in the fulfillment of natural laws. Secondly, Cedarquist's call for an aroused public to curb the excesses of the trust implies that such acts can be controlled to permit natural laws to operate more efficiently and with greater benefit. Norris, in other words, attributes to the railroad a conventional defense of its malpractices in order to demonstrate the falsity of that defense. Although Norris would accept Shelgrim's argument that the railroad and the farmer are inevitable forces which have risen to play necessary roles in the functioning of the law of supply and demand, he would deny Shelgrim's plea that individual railroads and individual farmers are not responsible for the ways in which they perform their roles. Presley is taken in by Shelgrim's defense because he has an incomplete awareness at this point of the relationship of individuals to moral law.

7. Lois Whitney, *Primitivism and the Idea of Progress in English Popular Literature of the Eighteenth Century* (Baltimore: Johns Hopkins Pr., 1934).

15—Jack London: The Problem of Form

1. I have been aided in my understanding of the fable by Marcel Gutwirth's published Mellon lecture, *Fable* (New Orleans: Graduate School of Tulane Univ., Fall, 1980), and by B. E. Perry's "Fable," *Studium Generale*, 12 (1959): 17–37.
2. Theodore Roosevelt, "Men Who Misinterpret Nature," in *The Works of Theodore Roosevelt* (New York: Scribner, 1926), V, 368–69; reprinted from *Everybody's Magazine*, 16 (June 1907): 770–74.
3. Earle Labor, "Jack London's *Mondo Cane: The Call of the Wild* and *White Fang*," *Jack London Newsletter*, 1 (July–Dec. 1967): 2–13; reprinted in Labor's *Jack London* (New York: Twayne, 1974), pp. 69–81.
4. London himself claimed, after the great success of *The Call of the Wild*, that he was unaware at the time he was writing the story that he was writing an allegory. But as to the allegorical nature of the completed work, he declared, "I plead guilty." See Joan London, *Jack London and His Times* (Seattle: Univ. of Washington Pr., 1968 [1939]), p. 252.
5. *Woman's Home Companion*, 33 (Sept. 1906): 5–7, 49.

16—Dreiser's "Nigger Jeff": The Development of an Aesthetic

1. I wish to thank the Curator of the Clifton Waller Barrett Library of the University of Virginia Library for permission to examine the manuscript and Mr. Harold J. Dies for permission to quote.
2. Dreiser told Richard Duffy, an editor of *Ainslee's Magazine*, that "Nigger Jeff" derived from a lynching he had seen during his St. Louis days. (Recalled by Duffy in a conversation with Robert H. Elias, Nov. 23, 1944. I wish to thank Professor Elias for

making his notes available to me.) T. D. Nostwich, in "The Source of Dreiser's, 'Nigger Jeff'," *Resources for American Literary Study*, 8 (Fall 1978): 174–87, has discovered and reprinted Dreiser's unsigned dispatches of Jan. 17–18, 1894, in the St. Louis *Republic* on the lynching. In the *Ainslee's* version of "Nigger Jeff," Dreiser shifted the date of the lynching from midwinter to early spring (he specified Apr. 16) for thematic reasons which I discuss below.

3. W. A. Swanberg, *Dreiser* (New York: Scribner, 1965), p. 58. Relying on Dreiser's account in *A Book About Myself* (New York: Boni and Liveright, 1922), Swanberg dates this trip as July. The chronology of Dreiser's contributions to the *Dispatch*, however, suggests early August as a more probable date.

4. Notes on Dreiser's lecture at Columbia University, Nov. 9, 1938 (in the possession of Robert H. Elias). See also Elias, *Theodore Dreiser: Apostle of Nature* (New York: Knopf, 1949), pp. 88, 317 n1.

5. Dreiser to H. L. Mencken, May 13, 1916, in *Letters of Theodore Dreiser*, ed. Robert H. Elias (Philadelphia: Univ. of Pennsylvania Pr., 1959), I, 212–13.

6. Swanberg, in *Dreiser*, p. 229, comments on Dreiser's extensive revision in the spring of 1918 of the stories making up the *Free* collection. It is of interest to note that critics have often quoted significant passages from the *Free* version and attributed them to the Dreiser of 1899 without realizing that these passages do not appear in the *Ainslee's* version. See, for example, F. O. Matthiessen, *Theodore Dreiser* (New York: Sloane, 1951), pp. 53–54.

7. The *Free* version contains a weak attempt to disguise the state. Pleasant Valley, Mo., becomes Pleasant Valley, Ko.

8. The name Eugene Davies has autobiographical implications, since Dreiser later used Eugene as the name of his autobiographical protagonist in *The "Genius."* In the *Free* "Nigger Jeff" Dreiser revised the reporter's name to Elmer Davies. *The "Genius"* had been published in 1915, which perhaps led Dreiser, in 1918, to consider Eugene as too explicitly autobiographical.

9. *Ainslee's Magazine*, 8 (Nov. 1901): 372. Citations hereafter appear in the text.

10. *Free and Other Stories* (New York: Boni and Liveright, 1918), p. 76. Citations hereafter appear in the text.

11. *The Stature of Theodore Dreiser*, ed. Alfred Kazin and Charles Shapiro (Bloomington: Indiana Univ. Pr., 1955) and Ellen Moers, "The Finesse of Dreiser," *American Scholar*, 33 (Winter 1963–1964): 109–14.

Selected Bibliography

The following list is restricted to specialized studies of late nine-teenth-century American intellectual and literary history, and to general studies of realism and naturalism which are relevant to late nineteenth-century American literature. It omits most standard surveys of American literature, fiction, and criticism, and criticism of individual authors and works. Many of the latter are referred to in the notes.

Books and Parts of Books

Ahnebrink, Lars. *The Beginnings of Naturalism in American Fiction*. Cambridge: Harvard Univ. Pr., 1950.

Auerbach, Erich. *Mimesis: The Representation of Reality in Western Literature*. Princeton: Princeton Univ. Pr., 1953.

Becker, George J. "Modern Realism as a Literary Movement," *Documents of Modern Literary Realism*, ed. George J. Becker. Princeton: Princeton Univ. Pr., 1963.

_____. *Realism in Modern Literature*. New York: Ungar, 1980.

Berthoff, Warner. *The Ferment of Realism: American Literature, 1884–1919*. New York: Free Pr., 1965.

Booth, Wayne C. *The Rhetoric of Fiction*. Chicago: Univ. of Chicago Pr., 1961.

Bowers, David F. "Hegel, Darwin, and the American Tradition," *Foreign Influences in American Life*, ed. David F. Bowers. Princeton: Princeton Univ. Pr., 1944.

Brooks, Van Wyck. *The Confident Years: 1885–1915*. New York: Dutton, 1952.

Cady, Edwin H. *The Light of Common Day: Realism in American Fiction*. Bloomington: Indiana Univ. Pr., 1971.

Cargill, Oscar. *Intellectual America: Ideas on the March*. New York: Macmillan, 1941.

Carter, Everett. *Howells and the Age of Realism*. Philadelphia: Lippincott, 1954.

Chase, Richard. *The American Novel and Its Tradition*. Garden City, N.Y.: Doubleday, 1957.

Cowley, Malcolm. "Naturalism in American Literature," *Evolutionary Thought in America*, ed. Stow Persons. New Haven: Yale Univ. Pr., 1950.

Falk, Robert P. "The Rise of Realism, 1871–91," *Transitions in American Literary History*, ed. Harry H. Clark. Durham, N.C.: Duke Univ. Pr., 1953.

———. "The Literary Criticism of the Genteel Decades: 1870–1900," *The Development of American Literary Criticism*, ed. Floyd Stovall. Chapel Hill: Univ. of North Carolina Pr., 1955.

———. "The Search for Reality: Writers and Their Literature," *The Gilded Age: A Reappraisal*, ed. H. Wayne Morgan. Syracuse: Syracuse Univ. Pr., 1963.

———. *The Victorian Mode in American Fiction, 1865–1885*. East Lansing: Michigan State Univ. Pr., 1965.

Farrell, James T. "Some Observations on Naturalism, So Called, in Fiction," *Reflections at Fifty and Other Essays*. New York: Vanguard, 1954.

Furst, Lilian, and Skrine, Peter N. *Naturalism*. London: Methuen, 1971.

Geismar, Maxwell. *Rebels and Ancestors: The American Novel, 1890–1915*. Boston: Houghton Mifflin, 1953.

Hakutani, Yoshinobu and Fried, Lewis, eds. *American Literary Naturalism: A Reassessment*. Heidelberg: Carl Winter, 1975.

Hofstadter, Richard. *Social Darwinism in American Thought, 1860–1915*. Philadelphia: Univ. of Pennsylvania Pr., 1945.

Jones, Howard M. *The Age of Energy: Varieties of American Experience, 1865–1915*. New York: Viking, 1971.

Kahn, Sholom J. *Science and Aesthetic Judgment: A Study in Taine's Critical Method*. New York: Columbia Univ. Pr., 1953.

Kazin, Alfred. *On Native Grounds*. New York: Reynal and Hitchcock, 1942.

_____. "American Naturalism: Reflections from Another era," *The American Writer and the European Tradition*, ed. Margaret Denny and William H. Gilman. Minneapolis: Univ. of Minnesota Pr., 1950.

Knight, Grant C. *The Critical Period in American Literature*. Chapel Hill: Univ. of North Carolina Pr., 1951.

Kolb, Harold H., Jr. *The Illusion of Life: American Realism as a Literary Form*. Charlottesville: Univ. Pr. of Virginia, 1969.

Levin, Harry. *The Gates of Horn: A Study of Five French Realists*. New York: Oxford Univ. Pr., 1963.

Lynn, Kenneth S. *The Dream of Success*. Boston: Little, Brown, 1955.

Martin, Jay. *Harvests of Change: American Literature, 1865–1914*. Englewood Cliffs, N.J.: Prentice-Hall, 1967.

Munro, Thomas. *Evolution in the Arts*. Cleveland: Cleveland Museum of Art, 1963.

Rahv, Philip. "Notes on the Decline of Naturalism," *Image and Idea*. Norfolk, Conn.: New Directions, 1949.

Stone, Edward, ed. *What Was Naturalism?: Materials for an Answer*. New York: Appleton-Century-Crofts, 1959.

Taylor, Walter F. *The Economic Novel in America*. Chapel Hill: Univ. of North Carolina Pr., 1942.

Trilling, Lionel. "Reality in America," *The Liberal Imagination*. New York: Viking, 1950.

Walcutt, Charles C. *American Literary Naturalism, A Divided Stream*. Minneapolis: Univ. of Minnesota Pr., 1956.

Watt, Ian. "Realism and the Novel Form," *The Rise of the Novel*. Berkeley: Univ. of California Pr., 1960.

Wellek, Rene. "The Concept of Evolution in Literary History," *Concepts of Criticism*. New Haven: Yale Univ. Pr., 1963.

_____. "The Concept of Realism in Literary Scholarship," *Concepts of Criticism*. New Haven: Yale Univ. Pr., 1963.

Williams, D. A., ed. *The Monster in the Mirror: Studies in Nineteenth-Century Realism*. Oxford: Oxford Univ. Pr., 1978.

Ziff, Larzer. *The American 1890s*. New York: Viking, 1966.

Articles

Bowron, Bernard R. "Realism in America," *Comparative Literature*, 3 (Summer 1951): 268–85.

Carter, Everett. "The Meaning of, and in, Realism," *Antioch Review*, 12 (Spring 1952): 78–94.

Clark, Harry H. "The Influence of Science on American Literary Criticism, 1860–1910 . . .," *Transactions of the Wisconsin Academy of Sciences, Arts, and Letters*, 44 (1955): 109–64.

Figg, Robert M. "Naturalism as a Literary Form," *Georgia Review*, 18 (Fall 1964): 308–16.

Greenwood, E. B. "Reflections on Professor Wellek's Concept of Realism," *Neophilologus*, 46 (Apr. 1962): 89–97.

Hoffman, Frederick J. "From Document to Symbol: Zola and American Naturalism," *Revue des Langues Vivantes*, U.S. Bicentennial Issue (1976): 203–12.

Levin, Harry. "What Is Realism?" *Comparative Literature*, 3 (Summer 1951): 193–99.

Meyer, George W. "The Original Social Purpose of the Naturalistic Novel," *Sewanee Review*, 50 (Oct. 1942): 563–70.

Peckham, Morse. "Darwinism and Darwinisticism," *Victorian Studies*, 3 (Sept. 1959): 19–40.

Randall, John H. "The Changing Impact of Darwin on Philosophy," *Journal of the History of Ideas*, 22 (Oct.–Dec. 1961): 435–62.

Wellek, René. "A Reply to E. B. Greenwood's Reflections," *Neophilologus*, 46 (July 1962): 194–96.

Williams, Raymond. "Realism and the Contemporary Novel," *Partisan Review*, 26 (Spring 1959): 200–13.

Index

Abrams, M. H., 3
—*Glossary of Literary Terms, A*, 3
Aeschylus, 75, 91
Aesop, 167, 171, 172
Ainslee's, 181, 182, 184, 187, 190
Arena, 135, 136
Arena Publishing Company, 135
Atlantic Monthly, 75, 134
Austen, Jane, 81

Balzac, Honoré de, 45, 78, 91
Baugh, Albert C., 87
—*Literary History of England, A*, 87
Beardsley, Aubrey, 114, 115
Becker, George J., 1–3, 9, 197 n.2
Bellow, Saul, 42, 120
Bewley, Marius, 154
Bible, 167, 171
Bohemianism, 115, 116
Boileau-Despréaux, Nicolas, 87
Boston Evening Transcript, 129
Boysesen, H. H., 87
Brown, Grace, 52
Browning, Robert, 62
Buckley, Jerome, 115
Byron, George Gordon, Lord, 29, 62

Cady, Edwin H., 31, 32, 40
—*Light of Common Day, The*, 31
Carter, Everett, 70–71
Century, 134, 136, 137
Chase, Richard, 9, 154
Chicago American, 107, 108
Christian Socialism, 124
Classicism, 78
Communist Party, 43, 46
Cooper, James Fenimore, 120
—*Leatherstocking Tales, The*, 3,
    Prairie, The, 119
Cowley, Malcolm, 43
—"Natural History of American
    Naturalism, A," 43
Crane, Stephen: naturalism in,
    9–12, 22–30, 31–40, 143–53;
    irony in, 23–25, 26–27, 143–53;
    symbolism in, 34–40; critical
    ideas of, 96–97, 102–106;
    impressionism in, 103–106;
    mentioned, xii, xiii, 41, 44, 110
—"Blue Hotel, The," 25, 27;
    "Bride Comes to Yellow Sky,
    The," 25; *Maggie: A Girl of the
    Streets*, xiv, 25, 103, 105, 106,
    143–53; "Open Boat, The," 25,

27; *Red Badge of Courage, The*, 12, 22–29, 35–40, 103, 104, 152
Critical realism, 71, 152

Darwin, Charles, 88, 94, 171
—*Origin of Species, The*, 86
Darwinism, 24, 40, 61, 88, 170, 203 n.1
Defoe, Daniel, 33
Democratic Party, 136
Dickens, Charles, 78
Dos Passos, John, 42
Dostoevsky, Feodor, 83
Dowden, Edward, 87, 93, 98
Dreiser, Theodore: naturalism in, 9–12, 17–22, 28–30, 31–40, 41–58, 59–60, 64–69; irony in, 18, 189; symbolism in, 21–22, 34–40; evolutionary ideas in, 66–67; critical ideas of, 180–93; mentioned, xii, 22, 110, 152, 153
—*American Tragedy, An*, 47, 52–58, 188, 191; *Book About Myself, A*, 182; *Bulwark, The*, 51, 189, 191, 192; *Dawn*, 188; *Financier, The*, 20; *Free and Other Stories*, 181, 182, 190, 191, 192, 214 n.6; *"Genius," The*, 214 n.8; *Hey-Rub-a-Dub-Dub*, 51, 182, 191, 192; *Jennie Gerhardt*, 20, 47–52, 57–58, 152; "Lynching of Nigger Jeff, The," 181, 187–88; "Nigger Jeff," 180–93; *Sister Carrie*, xii, 12, 17–22, 29, 35–40, 45, 46, 47, 64–69, 152, 182, 189; "Victim of Justice, A," 180–86 passim, 190, 192; "With the Nameless Dead," 181
Dryden, John, 87

Elias, Robert H., 180
Eliot, George: *Middlemarch*, 34, 39

Ellmann, Richard, 39
Emerson, Ralph Waldo, 101, 102
Enneking, John, 100
Evolutionary ideas: in criticism, xiii, 86–95, 203 n.1; in Norris, 14, 158–65; in Howells, 70–85; in Garland, 87, 89, 90, 92, 97–99, 129
Ev'ry Month, 181

Farmer's Alliance, 135
Farrell, James T., 42, 110
Faulkner, William, xiii, 39, 42, 44, 110, 114, 120
Fiedler, Leslie, 154
Fielding, Henry: *Tom Jones*, 5, 34
Fiske, John, 72, 75
Flower, B. O., 135

Garland, Hamlin: evolutionary ideas in, 87, 89–90, 92, 97–99, 129; critical ideas of, 96–102, 104–106; impressionism in, 99–102, 104; local color of, 127–42; mentioned, xiii, 72, 73, 74, 157
—"Among the Corn-Rows," 128, 134, 139; "Boy Life on the Prairie," 133, 137; "Branch-Road, A," 128, 134, 138, 139–140; *Crumbling Idols*, 97–102, 104; "Evolution of American Thought, The," 72, 90, 98; "John Boyle's Conclusion," 134; *Main-Travelled Roads*, 127–42; "Mrs. Ripley's Trip," 128, 134, 139; *Prairie Folks*, 134; "Prairie Heroine, A," 135; "Return of the Private, A," 128, 134, 139; *Rose of Dutcher's Coolly*, 136; *Son of the Middle Border, A*, 133; "Under the Lion's Paw," 128, 132, 134,

138, 139; *Under the Wheel,* 135;
"Up the Coulé," 128, 131, 132,
134, 138, 139–40
George, Henry, 131, 133, 136
—*Progress and Poverty,* 131
Gilder, Richard Watson, 136
Gillette, Chester, 52, 53
Goethe, Johann Wolfgang von, 79,
91
Grant, Ulysses S., 136–37

Haight, Gordon, 3
Harper's Monthly, 70, 134
Harper's Weekly, 134
Hawthorne, Nathaniel, xiii, 44,
78, 114, 155, 156, 184
—*Scarlet Letter, The,* 3, 34, 39
Hemingway, Ernest, 42, 120
Henley, William Ernest, 114, 115
Henry, Arthur, 181
Howe, E. W., 129
Howells, William Dean: realism
in, 1–8; critical ideas of, 70–85,
86–95 passim, 104–106;
evolutionary ideas in, 70–85,
86–95 passim; mentioned, 98,
101, 104, 107, 108, 129, 132,
135, 152, 157, 203 n.17
—*Annie Kilburn,* 126; *Criticism and
Fiction,* 70–85; "Editor's
Study," 70, 71, 76; *Rise of Silas
Lapham, The,* xiv, 2–8, 121–26;
Traveller from Altruria, A, 126
Hugo, Victor, 108, 109, 110
Huysmans, Joris Karl, 115

Ibsen, Henrik, 101
Impressionism: in Garland,
99–102, 104; in Crane, 103–106
Irony: in Dreiser, 18, 189; in
Crane, 23–25, 26–27, 143–53
Irving, Washington, 184

James, Henry: realism in, 1–8;
mentioned, xii, 44, 78, 118, 143
—*Tragic Muse, The,* 78; *What Maisie
Knew,* 2–8
James, William, 99
Jeffersonianism, 97
Joyce, James, 39
Jung, Carl, 169

Kazin, Alfred, 193
Kipling, Rudyard, 114, 115, 116,
163, 168, 174
—*Captains Courageous,* 115, 163;
Jungle Book, The, 168, 169; *Light
that Failed, The,* 115
Kirkland, Joseph, 129
Krutch, Joseph Wood, 29
—*Modern Temper, The,* 29

Labor, Earle, 169, 172
Lanier, Sidney, 86
Lawrence, D. H., 60
LeConte, Joseph, 158
*Literary History of the United States,
The,* 3
Local Color, 98–102, 127–42
London, Jack, 166–79
—"Apostate, The," 169, 173–74;
175; *Call of the Wild, The,* 168,
169, 170–72, 176; "Chinago,
The," 169, 172, 174; *Iron Heel,
The,* 169, 175; *John Barleycorn,*
170, 177–78, 179; *Martin Eden,*
170, 177–79; *Road, The,* 170,
177, 179; *Sea-Wolf, The,* 170,
175–77; "Strength of the Strong,
The," 169, 173, 174–75; "To
Build a Fire," 166, 169, 172–73,
174; *White Fang,* 168, 169,
170–72

McKinley, William, 136
Mailer, Norman, 120

Mann, Thomas, 60
Marcosson, Isaac, 110
Marx, Leo, 154–58, 162–65
—"Two Kingdoms of Force," 154
Marxism, 42
Matthews, Brander, 87
Melville, Herman, xiii, 44
—*Moby Dick,* 3, 40
Mill, John Stuart, 124–25, 210 n.8
Millet, Jean Francois, 141
Milton, John, 12
Modern Language Quarterly, 1
Moers, Ellen, 193

Naturalism: compared to realism,
    xi–xiii; in Dreiser, 9–12, 17–22,
    28–30, 31–40, 41–58, 59–60,
    64–69; in Norris, 9–17, 28–30,
    31–40, 59–64, 68–69; in Crane,
    9–12, 22–30, 31–40, 143–53;
    Norris's idea of, 107–11;
    mentioned, 198 n.2, 200 n.9
New York Tribune, 104
New York World, 53, 181
Nietzscheanism, 166
Nordau, Max, 115
—*Degeneration,* 115
Norris, Frank: primitivism of, xiii,
    112–20; naturalism in, 9–17,
    28–30, 31–40, 59–64; symbolism
    in, 39–40, 160–61; critical ideas
    of, 107–11, 112–20;
    evolutionary ideas in, 158–65;
    mentioned, xii, xiii, 22, 25, 41
—"Dying Fires," 116–20;
    McTeague, 12–17, 22, 29, 35–40,
    41, 110; *Octopus, The,* xiv, 110,
    154–65, 212 n.6; *Pit, The,*
    212 n.6; "Plea for Romantic
    Fiction, A," 107; *Vandover and the
    Brute,* 15, 61–64, 69; "Weekly
    Letter," 107, 108; "Zola as a
    Romantic Writer," 107, 109

Oliphant, Mrs. Margaret, 74
—*Literary History of England...,* 74

Parrington, V. L., 154
Pater, Walter, 115
Payne, William Morton, 87, 90,
    91, 94, 95
Peckham, Morse, 203 n.1
Pellew, George, 87
Perry, Bliss, 96
Perry, Thomas Sergeant, 72–76
    passim, 86–95 passim, 98,
    203 n.17
—*English Literature in the Eighteenth
    Century,* 73
Pittsburgh Dispatch, 181
Poe, Edgar Allan, 62
Pope, Alexander, 60
Populist Party, 135, 136, 142
Posnett, Hutcheson Macaulay,
    72–76 passim, 87–95 passim, 98,
    202 n.9
—*Comparative Literature,* 72, 76, 90,
    98
Pragmatism, 98–99
Primitivism: in Norris, xiii,
    112–20; mentioned, 4, 208 n.9

Rahv, Philip, 43
—"Notes on the Decline of
    American Naturalism," 43
Realism: compared to naturalism,
    xi–xiii; in Howells, 1–8; in
    James, 1–8; in Twain, 1–8;
    Howells's idea of, 77–78, 82–84;
    Norris's idea of, 107–11;
    mentioned, 31, 32, 70, 94, 103,
    114, 197 n.2
Republican Party, 136
Richardson, Samuel: *Pamela,* 34
Romanticism: Norris's idea of,
    107–11; mentioned, 24, 29, 31,
    32, 70, 78, 114

Roosevelt, Theodore, 168–69
Ruskin, John, 115

St. Louis Republic, 181
San Francisco *Wave*, 109
Scott, Sir Walter, 78, 91
Shakespeare, William, 75, 102
—*King Lear,* 53
Socialism, 116, 174
Sophocles, 75, 91
Spencer, Herbert, 45, 66, 72, 73,
    87, 88, 89, 98, 129, 171, 202 n.8
Spencerianism, 88, 89, 90, 92
Stedman, E. C., 86
Steinbeck, John, 42, 114, 120
Stevenson, Robert Louis, 114
Styron, William, 120
Swanberg, W. A., 180
Symbolism: in Dreiser, 21–22,
    35–40; in naturalism, 34–40; in
    Crane, 35–40, 103, 143–53; in
    Norris, 35–40, 160–61
Symonds, John Addington, 74, 76,
    86–95 passim
—*Renaissance in Italy,* 76

Taine, Hippolyte A., 72, 73, 75,
    77, 88, 89, 90
Taylor, W. F., 155, 157–58, 164
—*Economic Novel in America, The,*
    155
Thoreau, Henry David, 114, 155,
    156
Tolstoy, Count Leo, 126
Trevelyan, George M., 87
—*English Social History,* 87

Trilling, Lionel, 18, 43
—"Reality in America," 43
Twain, Mark: realism in, 1–8;
    mentioned, xii, 120, 156, 157
—*Adventures of Huckleberry Finn*, xii,
    2–8, 119, 156

Utilitarianism, 124–25, 210 n.8

Valdés, Armando, 101
Veritism, 101
Véron, Eugène, 99, 100
—*Aesthetics,* 99; *supériorité des arts
    modernes...,* La, 99

Walcutt, Charles C., 198 n.2
Walker, Franklin, 112
White, Sallie, 181
Whitman, Walt, 73, 102
Whitney, Lois, 162
Wilde, Oscar, 62, 114, 115, 116
—*De Profundis,* 115
Woolf, Virginia, 39
Wordsworth, William, 29

Yellow Book, 114

Zola, Émile, 51, 107, 108, 109,
    110, 144, 149, 163, 207 n.7
—*L'Assommoir,* 17, 144; *Débâcle,
    La,* 109, 207 n.9; *Fécondité,* 109,
    207 n.9; *Nana,* 144, 149; *Terre,
    La,* 109, 207 n.9
Zolaism, 33, 97, 107